THE HELLBLAZER

VOL. 2 THE SMOKELESS FIRE

THE HELLBLAZER
VOL. 2 THE SMOKELESS FIRE

SIMON OLIVER
writer

DAVIDE FABBRI * PHILIP TAN
JOSÉ MARZÁN JR. * KARL KESEL
artists

CARRIE STRACHAN * ELMER SANTOS
TONY AVIÑA
colorists

SAL CIPRIANO
letterer

YASMINE PUTRI
collection cover art

JOHN CASSADAY with PAUL MOUNTS
DECLAN SHALVEY with JORDIE BELLAIRE
RILEY ROSSMO
TULA LOTAY
original series covers

JOHN CONSTANTINE created by ALAN MOORE, STEVE BISSETTE,
JOHN TOTLEBEN and JAMIE DELANO & JOHN RIDGWAY

THE HELLBLAZER VOL. 2: THE SMOKELESS FIRE

DC Comics, 2900 West Alameda Ave., Burbank, CA 91505
Printed by LSC Communications, Kendallville, IN, USA. 9/22/17.
First Printing. ISBN: 978-1-4012-7389-7

Library of Congress Cataloging-in-Publication Data is available.

ARIS.

CROISSANT OR PAIN AU CHOCOLAT. ON THE FACE OF IT MIGHT BE A SIMPLE QUESTION, BUT IT SAYS A LOT ABOUT A PERSON...

LIKE PUTTING THE TEA BAG IN AFTER POURING THE WATER?

NO. THAT I CLASS A DEAL BREAKER...

LIKE HUMMING ALONG TO COLDPLAY?

MUSIC FOR BED WETTERS.

A LITTLE HARSH, MAYBE, BUT I'M NOT GOING TO ARGUE.

SO THIS GUY--HE DOES KNOW WE'RE COMING, DOESN'T HE?

OH, LOOK AT THAT, THERE'S THE EIFFEL TOWER.

WEIRD HOW IT ALWAYS SEEMS TO CREEP UP ON YOU LIKE THAT...

CONSTANTINE, DON'T CHANGE THE SUBJECT. I'M NOT ELEVEN ANYMORE.

WHO THE HELL IS THIS GUY WE'VE COME ALL THIS WAY TO SEE?

L' OCCIDENT PETROLEUM CO.
ARABIQUE SURVEYING EXPEDITION, 1936.

WITH THREE WEEKS BEHIND US, EACH STEP TAKES US FURTHER FROM WHAT I SO RECENTLY CONSIDERED CIVILIZATION.

THE SMOKELESS FIRE
PART 1

WRITER: SIMON OLIVER ARTIST: PHILIP TAN
COLORIST: ELMER SANTOS LETTERING: SAL CIPRIANO
COVER ARTIST: JOHN CASSADAY WITH PAUL MOUNTS
ASSOCIATE EDITOR: JESSICA CHEN
EDITOR: KRISTY QUINN
GROUP EDITOR: JIM CHADWICK

AND WHERE LAKES AND RIVERS ONCE FLOWED, OUR ROUTE TRACES THE INVISIBLE FOOTSTEPS OF THE FRANKINCENSE TRADERS WHO CAME BEFORE US...

...IN PURSUIT OF THE LIQUEFIED FOSSILS OF CREATURES WHO MILLIONS OF YEARS AGO ROAMED THESE VERY PLAINS.

ONWARDS WE WANDER, AS FAR AS ANY MAN DARE VENTURE...

...FAR BEYOND WHERE ANY WHITE MAN HAS EVER SET FOOT.

AND DEEPER INTO THE UNKNOWN...

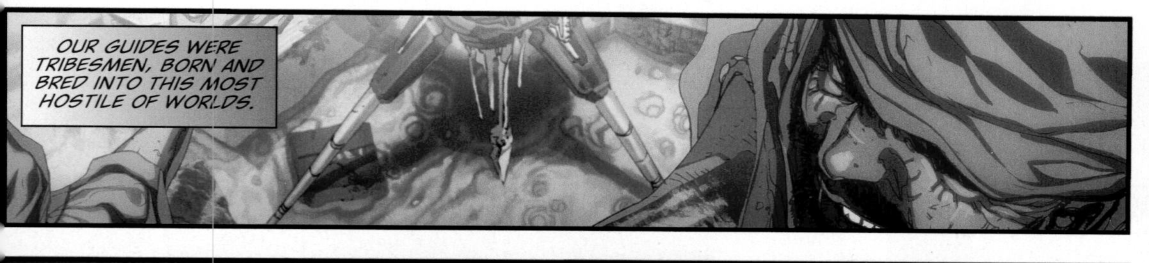

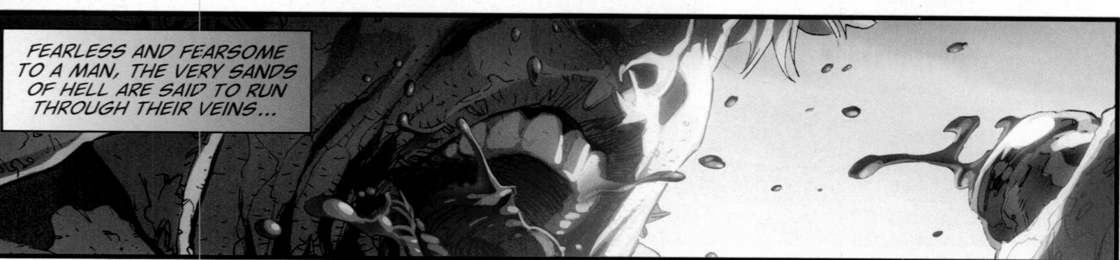

BEYOND SIMPLE ADMIRATION, AND DESPITE MY INITIAL NAIVE RESERVATIONS, I HAVE GROWN TO MARVEL AT THEIR CAPACITY FOR FORTITUDE, ENDURANCE, AND SILENCE IN THE FACE OF HARDSHIPS...

...HARDSHIPS THAT ONLY MONTHS BEFORE, BACK IN THE COMFORT OF MY NATIVE PARIS, I COULD NEVER HAVE BELIEVED, LET ALONE CONCEIVED...

CAREFUL WITH THOSE CASES...

...AND I HAVE GROWN TO TRUST THIS MOTLEY AND GRIZZLED TROUPE WITH NOTHING LESS THAN MY LIFE.

BUT AS MY COMFORT AND ACCEPTANCE OF THIS ALIEN ENVIRONMENT GROWS...
...WITH EACH STEP I SENSE A PALPABLE ANXIOUSNESS GROWING AMONGST OUR GUIDES.
BUT WHEREAS MY FEAR WAS A FEAR OF THE UNKNOWN, THEIRS WAS A FEAR OF THE KNOWN.
A FEAR BORNE OF A KNOWLEDGE PASSED DOWN BETWEEN GENERATIONS...
...A KNOWLEDGE OF WHAT THEY BELIEVE LIES IN WAIT FOR US IN THE RUB' AL KHALI.
AND A FEAR OF THE CREATURE THEY BELIEVE DWELLS DEEP BELOW THE SANDS RUNNING BENEATH OUR FEET.
A FEAR OF A CREATURE KNOWN BY THESE MEN AS THE DJINN.

SERIOUSLY, CONSTANTINE, WE CAME TO PARIS TO COLD-CALL SOME OLD GUY YOU MET YEARS AGO IN A DIVE BAR?
HE SEEMED LONELY, IT WAS JUST ANOTHER GHOST STORY...
...WHAT CAN I SAY? I'VE GOT ONE OF *THOSE* FACES, PEOPLE TELL ME ALL SORTS.
AND AS LONG AS THERE'S ENOUGH TO DRINK YOU'RE ONLY TOO HAPPY TO HEAR THEM OUT...

TOO RIGHT. THE BEST BOTTLE OF SINGLE MALT I EVER TASTED WAS UNCORKED BY SOMEONE TRYING TO SELL ME LOCH NESS MONSTER PUPS.
AND DID YOU BUY THEM?
COURSE NOT--EVERYONE KNOWS NESSIE HAS CALVES, NOT PUPS.
SHE DOES?

NO, MERCURY, DOESN'T...

...BECAUSE YOU'D HAVE TO BE ONE SANDWICH SHORT OF A PICNIC TO BELIEVE NESSIE WAS REAL.
SCREW YOU...
SORRY--COULDN'T HELP MYSELF.

WE'RE GONNA SEE THIS FELLA HENRY, HE'S GONNA TELL US HOW TO DEFEAT THE DJINN, YOU GET TO KEEP YOUR PROMISE TO THE JOLLY GREEN GIANT, GET ABBY BACK SAFELY TO THE ROT AND WE ALL LIVE HAPPILY EVER AFTER.

AND I PINKY PROMISE TO TRY AND BE LESS OF AN ARSEHOLE...
I'LL ADD THAT TO THE LIST OF "SIX IMPOSSIBLE THINGS TO BELIEVE BEFORE BREAKFAST."

MEANWHILE, ON THE OTHER SIDE OF PARIS...
NOW CARRY THE SEVEN...

...OVER TO THAT COLUMN THERE.
BUT I ALREADY DID THAT.
NO YOU DIDN'T, YOU PUT IT IN *THAT* COLUMN.
THAT'S NOT HOW THE TEACHER SHOWED US.
REALLY?
I'VE TOLD YOU THEY DON'T TEACH US PROPERLY.

AND I'VE TOLD YOU IT DOESN'T MATTER--YOU STILL HAVE TO GO TO SCHOOL.
IF IT'S SO IMPORTANT, WHY DO I HAVE TO AND *YOU* DON'T?

BECAUSE, MISS PUMPKINHEAD, ONE OF US HAS TO BE THE BRAINS OF THIS OPERATION.
KNOCK
KNOCK

WHO'S THAT?

NONE OF YOUR BEESWAX. CARRY THE SEVEN.

FIVE MINUTES LATER...
SO THIS OLD GUY'S APARTMENT, YOU'VE BEEN IN THERE?
I WORKED IN THE BUILDING, PAINTING AND DECORATING.
NO, BUT I'VE HEARD STORIES...
WHAT KIND OF STORIES?
THAT IT'S PACKED WITH ANTIQUES AND PAINTINGS AND ALL KINDS OF STUFF.

CASH?
I DON'T KNOW, BUT HE'S OLD AND CRAZY.
AND OLD AND CRAZY PEOPLE ALWAYS HAVE CASH LYING AROUND, DON'T THEY?

HERE'S THE ADDRESS.

NO...
...YOU WANT YOUR SHARE, YOU GOTTA EARN IT.
YOU'RE COMING WITH US...

AIN'T NOBODY IN THIS LIFE GONNA DO NOTHIN' FOR YOU...
...EXCEPT YOU.

WHERE ARE YOU GOING?
NONE OF YOUR--
"--BEESWAX..."
"I'LL BE LATE, DON'T WAIT UP."

"BUT YOU ARE COMING BACK, AREN'T YOU?"

"OF ***COURSE*** I'M COMING BACK.

"YOU DON'T THINK I'D EVER LEAVE MY PUMPKINHEAD ON HER OWN, DO YOU?"

WELCOME TO THE GANG, DANTE.

BETTER HOLD ON TIGHT...

"HAPPILY EVER AFTER" IS ALL VERY WELL, BUT WHAT DOES THAT MEAN TO JOHN CONSTANTINE?
I DIDN'T GO TO THIS MUCH TROUBLE TO COME BACK TO LONDON...
...ONLY TO GET RUN OUT ON MY HAIRY ARSE BY ALADDIN IN THE BLOODY LAMP.
NO, THIS TIME I GET TO GO HOME FOR GOOD.
VRRRRR
MERCURY! LOOK OUT--

MERCURY, YOU OKAY...?
I'M FINE. NOTHING BROKEN.

BLOODY HELL, YOU'VE GOT THAT LOOK...
...I REMEMBER THAT LOOK. YOU READ SOMEONE'S MIND...?
THIS OLD GUY WE'RE GOING TO SEE...
...WHERE DID YOU SAY HE LIVES?

WHY?
'CAUSE I'VE GOT A FEELING WE'RE NOT THE ONLY ONES ON OUR WAY TO SEE HIM.

MERCURY?

OÙ EST L'ARGENT?

WHAT DID YOU SAY?
I SAID I WAS WRONG. AND EVEN IF HE'S GOT ANY MONEY, HE AIN'T ABOUT TO TELL YOU...

REALLY? AND WHY YOU FIGURE THAT, SMART BOY?
'CAUSE HE AIN'T SCARED OF YOU.

ALL THIS YELLING AND SCREAMING? YOU'S AS GOOD AS TOLD 'IM YOU AIN'T GONNA PULL NO TRIGGER.
BUT YOU? YOU THINK YOU'RE GANGSTER ENOUGH...?
OR MAYBE YOU SPENT TOO MUCH TIME BABYSITTIN' LI'L SIS?

MAYBE WE SHOULD JUST LEAVE...

AND MAYBE BAPTISTE WAS RIGHT ALL ALONG...
...THAT IF WE TURNED OUR BACKS THESE BROWN SAVAGES WOULD SLIT OUR THROATS...

WHAT DID YOU CALL ME, OLD MAN?

COME ON...
...IF WE'RE NOT TOO LATE ALREADY.

IT'S LOCKED.
I'VE GOT THIS.

SOMEONE'S COMING UP.

DANTE, HE'S A CRAZY OLD MAN, HE DON'T KNOW WHAT HE'S SAYING, OR WHO YOU EVEN ARE...
BUT I DISAGREED...
WHERE'S THE MONEY?
YOU WERE MY NOBLE SAVAGES...
DANTE, THERE'S SOMEONE COMING--WE GOTTA GET OUT OF HERE...

...HE DON'T LOOK SO GOOD.
HERE IT COMES.
DEATH'S WARM EMBRACE...

COME ON...

I'LL CATCH YOU UP...

DANS CE LIVRE EST MA MÉMOIRE. GARDEZ-LE AVEC VOTRE VIE...

WHAT BOOK? WHAT ARE YOU TALKING ABOUT?
PLACE IT ON THE SCALES...

WHAT THE?
SHOOOSHHH

THAT'LL COME IN HANDY...

BLAMM BLAMM BLAMM BLAMM
⛧⛧⛧⛧, NO ONE SAID THERE'D BE GUNS...
CRRRS
HE'S GETTING AWAY.
NO ⛧⛧⛧⛧, SHERLOCK.

MERCURY, YOU EVER DO SAINT JOHN'S AMBULANCE?
NO, TWO WEEKS IN THE GIRL GUIDES. WHY?
BECAUSE YOU'RE GONNA HAVE TO SAVE THE ONE MAN I KNOW WHO KNOWS ANYTHING ABOUT GENIES.

?!
AND WHAT ABOUT YOU?

WHERE THE HELL DID HE GO?

QUI DIABLE ÊTES-VOUS?
JUST SOME ARSEHOLE...
...TALK

LET'S NOT BE HASTY NOW--MAYBE WE CAN...
LES MAINS EN L'AIR.
MERCURY, IF THE OLD MAN'S BROWN BREAD, I REALLY DON'T WANT TO BE HERE WHEN THE *GENDARMES* SHOW UP...
...MERCURY?

YOU CAME BACK!
YOU KNOW I'LL NEVER LEAVE YOU, PUMPKINHEAD...
A FEAR OF THE CREATURE THEY BELIEVE DWELLS DEEP BELOW THE SANDS RUNNING BENEATH OUR FEET.
A FEAR OF A CREATURE KNOWN BY THESE MEN AS THE DJINN.
WHAT LIES AHEAD, OF THAT I NEVER BEEN MORE UNSURE.
BUT ONE DAY, THE TESTAMENT WITHIN THIS HUMBLE JOURNAL MAY BE ALL THAT IS LEFT TO TELL MY TALE.

L' OCCIDENT PETROLEUM CO.
ARABIQUE EXPEDITION, 1936.
THE DESERT WAS NOT WHAT I IMAGINED FROM THE COMFORTABLE CONFINES OF THE READING ROOMS OF THE SORBONNE.
LE CHEVAL... IT IS SICK.
IT WAS HARSH AND UNYIELDING, BARREN AND NEAR LIFELESS, BUT AT THE SAME TIME SO MUCH MORE.
AND WITH EACH PASSING STEP DEEPER INTO ITS HEART, ITS TRUE NATURE BEGAN TO REVEAL ITSELF...
...LESS A PHYSICAL PLACE AND MORE A REFLECTION, A MIRROR HELD UP TO THOSE OF US WHO DARED TRAVEL WITHIN IT.
FOR ALL HIS FAULTS, AND HE HAD MANY, I BELIEVE BAPTISTE HAD LONG KNOWN WHAT I WAS ONLY JUST BEGINNING TO GRASP.
AND WITH NOTHING LEFT TO DISCOVER, ONWARD BAPTISTE MARCHED, PUSHING US ON, AS ACCOMPLICES AND WITNESSES TO A FATE THAT SEEMED ALL BUT SEALED.
SPREAD OUT THE REMAINING PACKS.
BLAMMM
THE ONLY QUESTION LEFT IN MY MIND WAS WHAT FINAL FATE THE DESERT MIGHT HAVE IN STORE FOR ME...

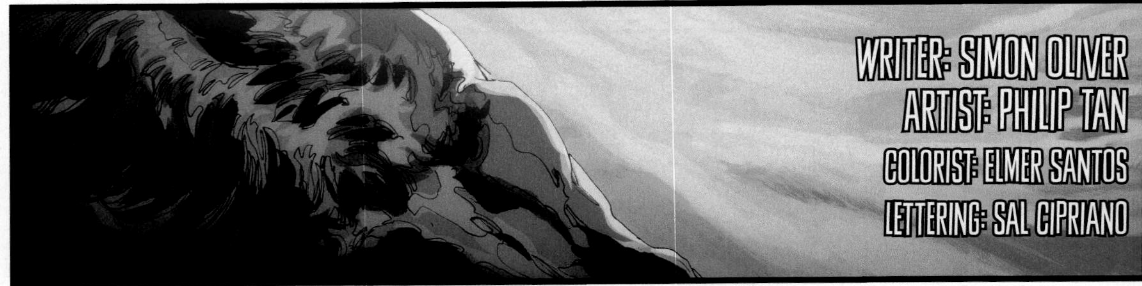

COVER ARTIST: DECLAN SHALVEY WITH JORDIE BELLAIRE
ASSOCIATE EDITOR: JESSICA CHEN EDITOR: KRISTY QUINN
GROUP EDITOR: JIM CHADWICK

PARLEZ-VOUS FRANÇAIS, MONSIEUR CONSTANTINE?

MAIS BLOODY QUI...

PARIS. PRESENT DAY.
QUE FAISIEZ-VOUS À LA MAISON, MONSIEUR CONSTANTINE?

BIEN SÛR, MON PLEASURE MONSIEUR DÉTECTIVE.
<VERY GOOD. SO WHY WERE YOU AT THE HOUSE, MISTER CONSTANTINE?>

LE VENDEUR DE GLACÉE...
...EST DERRIÈRE LA GRILLE.
<WHAT IS HE TALKING ABOUT?>

<HE SAID "THE ICE-CREAM SALESMAN IS BEHIND THE RAILING?">

IL EST UN IMBÉCILE...

NOW THE QUESTION IS, WHERE THE HELL HAS MERCURY GOT TO?

YOU'VE ALWAYS WONDERED.
WHY YOU WERE DIFFERENT.
WHY YOU F ALL PEOPLE VERE GIVEN THIS GIFT.
BUT YOU DON'T KNOW THE REASON-- DO YOU, MERCURY?

YOU *REALLY* DON'T KNOW WHOSE FOOTSTEPS YOU FOLLOW IN?
ISN'T THAT WHY I'M HERE? AND WHY YOU'RE HERE? ADNAN, YOU PROMISED ME ANSWERS...

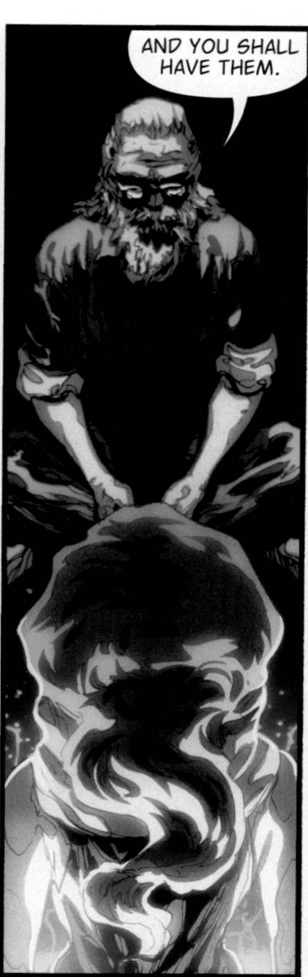
AND YOU SHALL HAVE THEM.

YOUR ABILITIES TO HEAR THINGS OTHERS CANNOT, TO SEE AND TRAVEL BEYOND WHAT IS KNOWN...THOSE YOU HAVE LONG KNOWN ABOUT.

BUT, MERCURY, THERE'S MORE, SO MUCH MORE TO WHAT YOU CAN DO...
TELL ME WHAT I CAN DO.
TELL ME WHAT I AM.
YOU AND YOU ALONE COULD MASTER CONTROL OVER MY KIND...

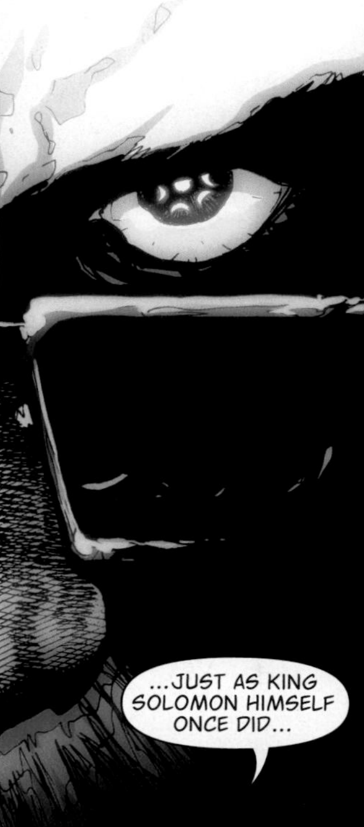
...JUST AS KING SOLOMON HIMSELF ONCE DID...

KING SOLOMON?
YES, KING SOLOMON HIMSELF.
AND WITH MY HELP YOU WILL FOLLOW IN HIS FOOTSTEPS...
AND WHAT DO YOU GET, EXACTLY, FOR HELPING ME?
TO SERVE AT YOUR SIDE, JUST AS I ONCE SERVED AT HIS.
TO BE MY GENIE IN A BOTTLE?
IF THAT IS WHAT YOU WISH, THEN IT WILL BE SO.
BUT FIRST, A WORD OF WARNING. THAT MAN YOU ARE WITH...
...HE IS NOT TO BE TRUSTED.
STOP THE BLOODY PRESSES...
AND FOR ONCE CAN SOMEON TELL ME SOMETHIN I DON'T KNOW ABOUT JOHN CONSTANTINE?

IF HE DISCOVERS WHAT YOU CAN DO, WHAT YOU ARE CAPABLE OF--
MADEMOISELLE MERCURY...?
I HAVE TO GO.
MADEMOISELLE MERCURY... OÙ ES-TU?
YOU CAN'T TELL CONSTANTINE ABOUT OUR LITTLE ARRANGEMENT.
MADEMOISELLE MERCURY...?

UTILIT
MADEMOISELLE MERCURY...?
RIGHT HERE, JUST STEPPED OUT TO FRESHEN UP.

HMM?

YOUR FRIEND MONSIEUR CONSTANTINE--YOU CAN, HOW YOU SAY IN ENGLISH... "BAIL HIS ARSE OUT"?
I THINK YOU MIGHT WANT TO TAKE IT EASY ON THE COP SHOWS.

YOU TOOK YER TIME. WHAT DID YOU DO, POP OUT AND GET YER BLOODY NAILS DONE?
WATCH IT, CONSTANTINE.
'CAUSE A LITTLE *PAPILLON*-STYLE SELF-REFLECTION MIGHT BE JUST WHAT THE DOCTOR ORDERED.
SIGN 'ERE AND 'ERE.
AND FOR THE REST OF YOUR TIME IN PARIS, PLEASE KEEP HIM OUT OF TROUBLE...?
WHAT IS IT, JOHN?
MORE LIKE "WHO IS IT"?
SHE'S BEEN HERE SINCE I GOT HERE. HENRY'S DAUGHTER...
...HE DIDN'T HAVE A DAUGHTER... DID HE?
NOT THAT THE LIGHTNESS OF HIS LOAFERS STOPPED OSCAR WILDE FROM POPPING OUT TWO...
...BUT IF HENRY HAS A DAUGHTER, THAT'S NOT HER.
SO, YOU SIGNING OR AM I PUTTING 'IM BACK IN ZEE "SLAMMER"?
SHE'S SIGNING.

I'M JUST SAYING--YOU OF ALL PEOPLE SHOULDN'T BE SO CLOSED-MINDED.
HOW ABOUT 'E HAVE THIS ONVERSATION ANOTHER TIME? AS IN NEVER...
FOLLOW THAT CAB...
YOU KNOW HER, DON'T YOU?
GOES BY THE NAME OF MADEMOISELLE MISABEL LEFEBVRE...
AND HOW DOES SHE PAY THE RENT?
OFFICIALLY, A DEALER IN ANTIQUITIES.
AND UNOFFICIALLY?
POLICE
SHE SPECIALIZES IN BLACK-MARKET SPIRITUAL CURIOSITIES OF A DISTINCTLY ETHNIC NATURE...
...DABBLES IN THE DARKER HANDICRAFTS AND "THINGS" THAT GO BUMP IN THE NIGHT.
AND FOR FUN?
YOU DON'T WANT TO KNOW...
SOUNDS LIKE AN INTERESTING TINDER PROFILE.

MISABEL'S APPEARANCE IS USUALLY AN ACCURATE HARBINGER OF TROUBLE ON THE HORIZON.
COMING FROM YOU I TAKE THAT AS...
...TROUBLING.
BECAUSE I'M GETTING THE DISTINCT IMPRESSION THAT SHE'S GOT AT LEAST ONE OVER ON YOU IN THE PAST.
LET'S JUST SAY IT WENT TO PENALTIES.
THAT MEANS YOU LOST.
SO THIS SHOULD AT LEAST BE INTERESTING.
WHERE IS IT? WHERE THE HELL IS IT?
LOOKING FOR SOMETHING, MISABEL?
JOHN BLOODY CONSTANTINE?
I SHOULD HAVE KNOWN.

WHEN THEY SAID THEY'D ARRESTED SOME FOUL-MOUTHED ENGLISH LOUT I SHOULD HAVE PUT TWO AND TWO TOGETHER.
AND COME UP "QUATRE"?
VERY GOOD--MAYBE IF YOUR FELLOW COUNTRYMEN WERE AS "CONTINENTAL" AND BROAD-MINDED, BREXIT WOULD HAVE NEVER SEEN THE LIGHT OF DAY.

YOU KNOW ME. AS EVERYONE'S FAVORITE PEDO-STONE ONCE SAID, "JE SUIS UN ROCK STAR" AND ALL THAT.
AND TO THINK, THE JOHN CONSTANTINE I KNOW IS JUST A HUMBLE MAGICIAN.

AS USUAL YOU'RE BEING TOO KIND, MISABEL.
IN DESCRIBING YOU AS "HUMBLE" OR A "MAGICIAN"?

IT'S A TOSS-UP. TAKE YOUR PICK...
OH, AND WHO'S THIS?
HAVE YOU PICKED YOURSELF UP A LITTLE SIDEKICK?
WOW, YOU WEREN'T JOKING. SHE'S ALREADY PISSING ME OFF.

YOU *DO* KNOW WHAT FATE USUALLY BEFALLS HIS POOR ASSOCIATES?
FOR CHRIST'S SAKE, WOULD SOMEONE JUST ONCE TELL ME SOMETHING I DON'T KNOW ABOUT HIM...

MAYBE YOU'D LIKE TO TELL ME EXACTLY WHAT YOU'RE DOING HERE?
I ASKED FIRST...

NO, I'M PRETTY SURE YOU DIDN'T.
AND ANYWAY, WHY ON EARTH WOULD I TELL YOU ANYTHING?
WELL I'M BETTING WHATEVER SHE'S LOOKING FOR--

THE KID TOOK WITH HIM.
WHAT KID? YOU SAW HIM?

YOU SAID IT YOURSELF. "WHY ON EARTH WOULD I TELL YOU ANYTHING?"
BECAUSE YOU DON'T KNOW WHAT THEY TOOK, DO YOU?

JUST LIKE YOU HAVE NO IDEA WHERE HE WENT.
AND *YOU* DO?

NOT YET, BUT I WILL.
HOW?
YOU SAID IT YOURSELF--I'M JUST A "HUMBLE MAGICIAN."
A HUMBLE MAGICIAN WHOM I'M GUESSING IS ABOUT TO MAKE ME A PROPOSITION I CAN'T REFUSE?
IT WOULDN'T BE THE FIRST TIME WE'VE BEEN STRANGE BEDFELLOWS, NOW WOULD IT...?
JESUS, GET A ROOM WHY DON'T YOU.

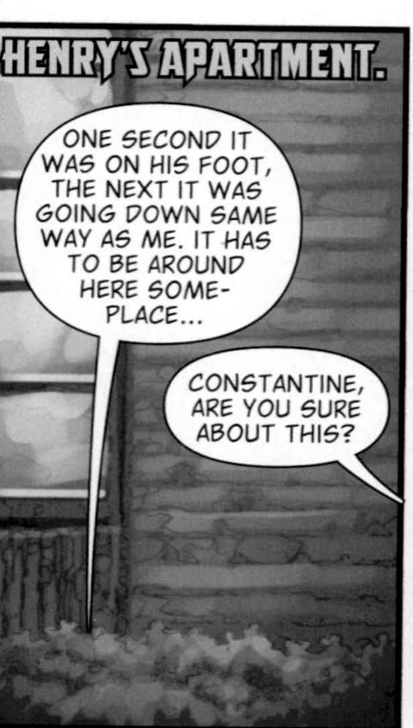
HENRY'S APARTMENT.
ONE SECOND IT WAS ON HIS FOOT, THE NEXT IT WAS GOING DOWN SAME WAY AS ME. IT HAS TO BE AROUND HERE SOME-PLACE...
CONSTANTINE, ARE YOU SURE ABOUT THIS?

WE STRING FRENCHY SPICE ALONG AND WHEN WE'VE GOT WHAT WE NEED, GIVE HER THE SLIP.

THERE IT IS...

I WAS ACTUALLY MORE CONCERNED ABOUT THE MAGIC PART OF YOUR MASTER PLAN.
MERCURY, YOU WORRY TOO MUCH.

BACK THERE, WHAT YOU SAID... SOMEONE BEEN WHISPERING IN YOUR SHELL-LIKE EAR?
COME ON, YOUR REPUTATION? IT'S NOT EXACTLY BREAKING NEWS, NOW IS IT?
BAD THINGS HAPPEN TO PEOPLE AROUND YOU.

MERCURY, THIS IS DIFFERENT. WE HAVE HISTORY.
...AND NO MATTER WHAT, I'VE GOT YOUR BACK.
MAYBE YOU NEED TO ASK YOURSELF HOW MANY TIMES YOU'VE SAID THAT.

SO, SIDEKICK, WHAT'S YOUR PARTY TRICK?

WHO SAYS I HAVE ONE?

QUANTUS TREMOR EST FUTURUS,

QUANDO IUDEX EST VENTURUS,

CUNCTA STRICTE DISCUSSURUS!

BECAUSE IF YOU DON'T, I, FOR ONE, WOULD LIKE TO KNOW WHAT YOU'RE DOING HERE.

TUBA MIRUM SPARGENS SONUM,

PER SEPULCRA REGIONUM,

COGET OMNES ANTE THRONUM.

RISE-US NIKES-US...

WELL CONSTANTINE, LOOKS LIKE THE DEAL IS OFF.

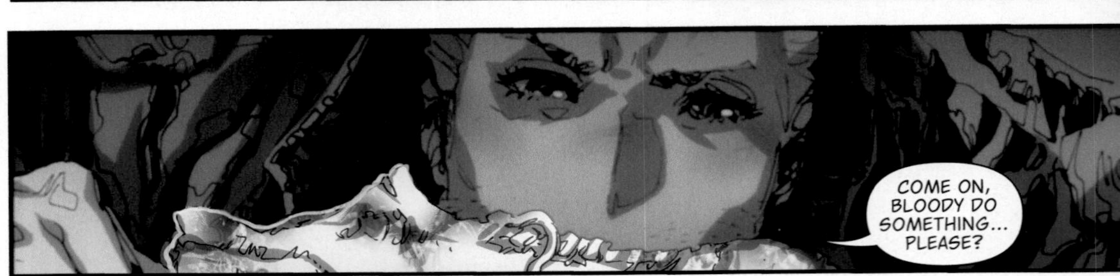

JUST ONE WORD FROM ME WILL COMPLETE THE SPELL...

...AND THE SHOE WILL LEAD US BACK TO ITS OWNER.

MON DIEU!

MON BLOODY *DIEU* EXACTLY. FORGET I EVER DOUBTED YOU, CONSTANTINE.

BUT FIRST--WE HAD A DEAL, MISABEL.

DON'T WORRY--
IT'S NOT GOING
ANYWHERE. NOT
UNTIL I TELL
IT.
CONSTANTINE!

REALLY? BECAUSE IT
CERTAINLY LOOKS LIKE IT
HAS OTHER PLANS.
THE JOURNAL?
WHAT'S IN IT THAT'S
SO IMPORTANT?

SANS
COMMENTAIRES.
WHO ARE
YOU WORKING
FOR...?

CRASH
AS ALWAYS,
IT WOULD APPEAR
YOU'VE OVERPLAYED
YOUR HAND,
CONSTANTINE.

THE TRIBESMEN SAID THAT
NCE YOU PASSED THE POINT
OF NO RETURN, THEN
WHATEVER LAY AHEAD WAS
IN THE HANDS OF ALLAH.

AND I BELIEVED THEM, FOR
THE DESERT WASN'T A PLACE
FOR LIES, ONLY TRUTH...

...A PLACE WHERE
DREAMS WERE TAKEN,
NEVER TO RETURN...

...WHERE YOU WERE
STRIPPED OF BELIEF
AND LEFT ONLY WITH
WHAT YOU FEARED.
HENRY

QUI ÊTES-VOUS?

WHAT DO YOU WANT FROM ME?

HENRY!

COME, IT IS NOT SAFE OUT HERE...

WHO KNOWS WHAT LAY BEYOND--AND IF FARRAJ HADN'T FOLLOWED ME, WHAT FATE HAD IN STORE?
THEY SAID THOSE WHO WANDERED TO NEVER RETURN BECAME A PART OF THE CLOUDS ABOVE THEIR HEADS, A PART OF THE SAND BENEATH THEIR FEET.

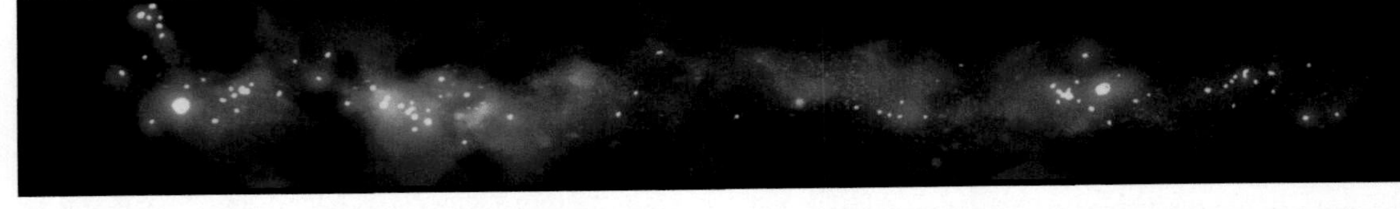

THAT THEY BECAME A PART OF EVERYTHING AND NOTHING.

QUI ÊTES-VOUS?

WHO'S THERE?

DANTE, I COULDN'T SLEEP...

CAN I STAY IN HERE WITH YOU TONIGHT?
THE BOOK, CAN YOU READ SOME OF IT TO ME?
?!!

O, IT'S OT FOR KIDS.

IT MUST BE SCARY, 'CAUSE YOUR HEART IS BEATING REALLY, REALLY FAST.

JUST REMEMBER WHAT YOU SAY TO ME WHEN I GET SCARED WATCHING TV-- "IT'S NOT REAL."
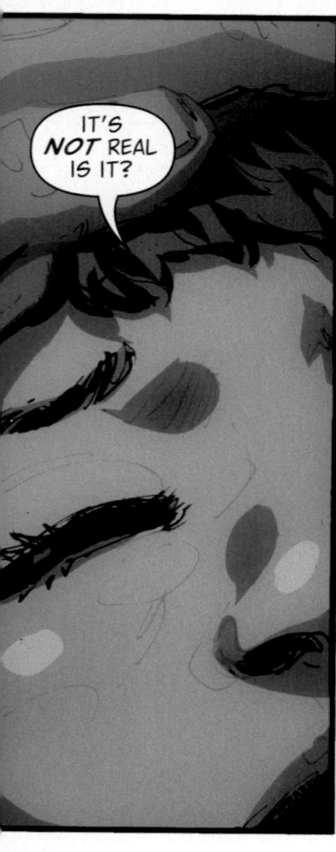
IT'S ***NOT*** REAL IS IT?

NO, IT'S JUST A BOOK.

NONE OF IT'S REAL.

FOLLOW THAT SHOE!

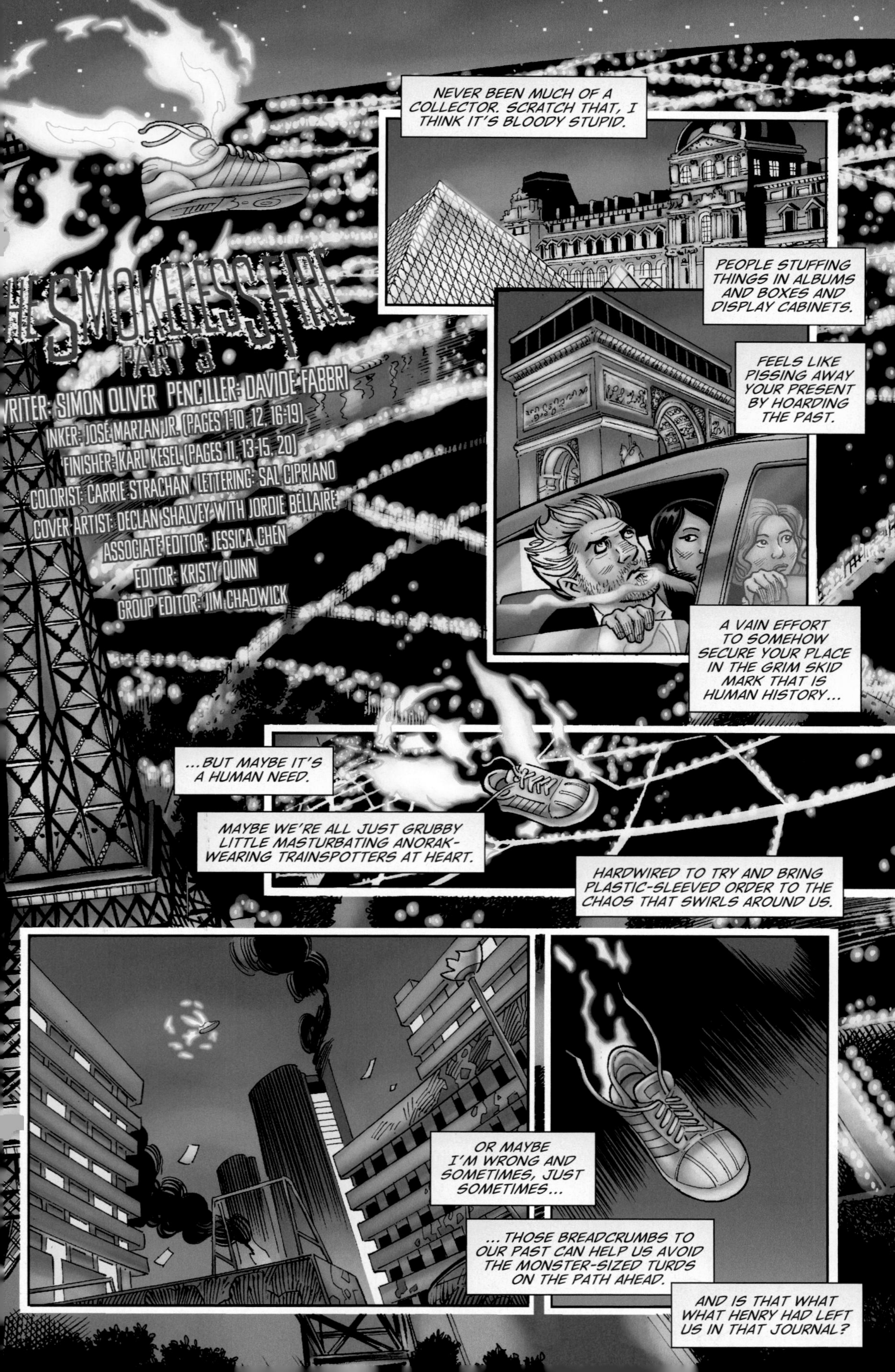
SMOKELESS FIRE
PART 3
RITER: SIMON OLIVER PENCILLER: DAVIDE FABBRI
INKER: JOSÉ MARZAN JR. (PAGES 1-10, 12, 16-19)
FINISHER: KARL KESEL (PAGES 11, 13-15, 20)
COLORIST: CARRIE STRACHAN LETTERING: SAL CIPRIANO
COVER ARTIST: DECLAN SHALVEY WITH JORDIE BELLAIRE
ASSOCIATE EDITOR: JESSICA CHEN
EDITOR: KRISTY QUINN
GROUP EDITOR: JIM CHADWICK
NEVER BEEN MUCH OF A COLLECTOR. SCRATCH THAT, I THINK IT'S BLOODY STUPID.
PEOPLE STUFFING THINGS IN ALBUMS AND BOXES AND DISPLAY CABINETS.
FEELS LIKE PISSING AWAY YOUR PRESENT BY HOARDING THE PAST.
A VAIN EFFORT TO SOMEHOW SECURE YOUR PLACE IN THE GRIM SKID MARK THAT IS HUMAN HISTORY...
...BUT MAYBE IT'S A HUMAN NEED.
MAYBE WE'RE ALL JUST GRUBBY LITTLE MASTURBATING ANORAK-WEARING TRAINSPOTTERS AT HEART.
HARDWIRED TO TRY AND BRING PLASTIC-SLEEVED ORDER TO THE CHAOS THAT SWIRLS AROUND US.
OR MAYBE I'M WRONG AND SOMETIMES, JUST SOMETIMES...
...THOSE BREADCRUMBS TO OUR PAST CAN HELP US AVOID THE MONSTER-SIZED TURDS ON THE PATH AHEAD.
AND IS THAT WHAT WHAT HENRY HAD LEFT US IN THAT JOURNAL?

CE QUI LA BAISE?

EXCUSEZ-MOI, BUT I THINK THAT'S MINE...

AU REVOIR, JEAN CONSTANTINE...
DO YOUR "THING," READ HER MIND--FIND OUT WHERE SHE'S GOING!
YOU KNOW IT DOESN'T WORK LIKE THAT. I'M NOT SOME KIND OF BLOODY PSYCHIC POLICE SCANNER...
NOT THAT I'M NOT GRATEFUL FOR GETTING ME THIS FAR, CONSTANTINE, BUT WE HAD AN ARRANGEMENT AND NOW THAT ARRANGEMENT IS OVER...
WE NEED TO TALK...ABOUT WHAT THE KID STOLE FROM HENRY'S HOUSE...
...THE JOURNAL. HENRY'S JOURNAL, WHAT'S SO IMPORTANT ABOUT IT?
A MAN YOUR AGE, YOU SHOULD REALLY BE SPENDING LESS TIME THINKING ABOUT THE *PAST* AND MORE TIME THINKING ABOUT WHAT LITTLE TIME YOU HAVE *LEFT*.
ALSO THINK ABOUT CUTTING DOWN ON THE FAGS AND BOOZE.
SLOW DOWN...
...WHO SENT YOU?
POOR LITTLE JEAN. EVEN IF YOU FIND OUT, WHICH I DOUBT...
...IT WILL BE TOO LATE.
SHE MIGHT HAVE A POINT.
YOU KNOW, ABOUT THE FAGS AND BOOZE.
THANKS.

SO NOW ALL WE HAVE TO DO IS FIND THE SHOELESS THIEF WHO KICKED YOU OFF THE ROOF BEFORE YOUR GIRLFRIEND DOES.
BARKING UP THE WRONG TREE THERE.
ME AND MISABEL? I WOULDN'T, NOT EVEN WITH YOURS...
AND I'M NOT EVEN GOING TO PRETEND TO KNOW WHAT THAT MEANS.
IT'S AN EXPRESSION.
I'M GUESSING LAST USED BEFORE WE WENT DECIMAL.
AND NOW WE'RE LEFT PLAYING SECOND FIDDLE TO THE SKIRT-WEARING, BETTER-SMELLING FRENCH VERSION OF YOU.
DID YOU JUST SAY THE "FRENCH VERSION" OF ME?
YOU SERIOUSLY THINK ME AND THAT COLD-HEARTED MERCENARY HAVE ANYTHING IN COMMON?
NO, SORRY, YOU'RE RIGHT...
...UNLIKE YOU, SHE'S NOT JUST POWER HUNGRY--SHE'S AMBITIOUS, AND ABOVE ALL, COMPETENT.
AND SOMEHOW THAT'S SUPPOSED TO MAKE ME FEEL BETTER?
NO WITTY RETORT?
WHAT IS IT?

MAYBE WHOEVER SENT MISABEL DOESN'T ACTUALLY NEED WHAT'S IN THE JOURNAL.
MAYBE SHE'S BEEN SENT TO STOP ANYONE ELSE GETTING THEIR GRUBBY LITTLE HANDS ON IT?
EXACTLY. BECAUSE HENRY'S JOURNAL MIGHT BE THE ONLY KNOWN ROUTE TO UBAR AND ABBY.
AND IF I WERE A THIEF WITH A STOLEN JOURNAL--
I'D BE GOING HELL-FOR-LEATHER TO GET IT OFF MY HANDS.
MEANWHILE IN LONDON, ENGLAND.
...SO DOES ANYONE WANT TO TELL ME WHAT THE ⊗⊗⊗⊗ IS GOING ON IN THERE?
DO NONE OF YOU WORTHLESS SPECIMENS HAVE THE BALLS TO ENLIGHTEN ME?
THE HOUSES OF PARLIAMENT--MAJORITY PARTY CHAMBERS.

BECAUSE NO ONE'S GOING HOME TO "HER INDOORS" AND THE TWO-POINT-FIVE SNOTTY-NOSED RUGRATS UNTIL YOU DRAG YOUR SORRY ARSES BACK IN THERE AND VOTE LIKE YOU'VE BEEN TOLD.
AM I CLEAR?
WHAT ABOUT THE PRIME MINISTER, MR. CARVER?
WHAT *ABOUT* THE PRIME MINISTER?
WELL, WHAT DOES SHE THINK?
WITH ALL DUE RESPECT, THE RIGHT HONORABLE PRIME MINISTER MIGHT BE ONE STEP ABOVE YOU SIGHTLESS GRUBS ON THE EVOLUTIONARY LADDER...
...BUT IN ANSWER TO YOUR QUESTION, THE PRIME MINISTER WILL THINK WHATEVE I WANT HER TO BLEEDING THINK.

BECAUSE I DON'T ***WANT*** THE BLOODY TRAINS TO RUN ON TIME. THAT'S WHY!
BECAUSE IF THEY DID, PEOPLE MIGHT START LOOKING AROUND AND WONDER WHY NOTHING ***ELSE*** IN THIS BLOODY COUNTRY WORKS.
AND THEN GOD FORBID YOU MIGHT START HAVING TO GET SOMETHING DONE.
AND WE WOULDN'T WANT THAT, NOW WOULD WE?
HE TATE CLUB.
MEMBERS ONLY
MR. CARVER, YOU'RE FASHIONABLY LATE.
"TROUBLE AT T' MILL" SO TO SPEAK. THE NATIVES NEEDED PUTTING IN THEIR PLACES.
SO I HEARD--AND OF COURSE MADE THE APPROPRIATE ARRANGEMENTS FOR YOUR EVENING WITH US.
YOUR USUAL ROOM AND REQUIREMENTS ARE READY AND WAITING.

CLARICE, IF I'VE NEVER SAID IT BEFORE--AND NOW THAT I THINK OF IT I DON'T THINK I EVER HAVE.
NOT TO ANYONE.
BUT YOU'RE ONE OF THE VERY, VERY FEW PEOPLE I CAN TRUST TO DO THE RIGHT THING.
AS ALWAYS, YOU'RE TOO KIND...

GIVE HIM A MINUTE.
THAT'S WHAT I LIKE ABOUT YOU, CLARICE...
...THOUGHTFUL AND CONSIDERATE, RIGHT UP UNTIL THE END.
JUST BREATHE...
...AND LET T
MARSHMALLO
CLOUDS CAR
YOU AWAY.
WOOO... HERE IT COMES.

RETOUR, DANS LA VILLE DE LA LUMIÈRE.
BOLLYWOOD
BOLLYWOOD
JE SUIS CHERCHE POR UNE JOURNAL, TRES, TRES OLD.
ANTIQUITÉS
HOTEL
le Pavilla

UN JOURNAL. YOU KNOW, "LA LIBRE" BUT YOU WRITE IN IT, AND SOMEONE BROUGHT IT IN?
UN LIBRE?
YES, YES, "LA LIBRE" BUT VERY, TRES OLD...JOHN, DO YOU KNOW HOW THEY SAY "OLD"?
"VIEUX" IS OLD.

YES, "UN VIEUX JOURNAL"...
...YOU DON'T BY CHANCE HAVE ANYTHING LIKE THAT? DO YOU?
OUI, BIEN SÛR... PAR ICI.

JOHN, HE SAYS HE HAS IT.

COME, COME... THIS WAY.
MAYBE HE KEEPS THE GOOD STUFF IN THE BACK.

YOU SEE MANY, MANY OLD "JOURNALS."
WOOOWW...

OLD BOOKS, YES?
IS THIS NOT WHAT YOU WANTED?
COMIC BOOKS ARE NOT EXACTLY WHAT I HAD IN MIND...
WOW, YOU CAN ALMOST TASTE THE PAIN AND SUFFERING IN THESE...
VICTORIAN
LOOK AT THAT--IS JOHN CONSTANTINE GETTING IN TOUCH WITH HIS INNER NERD?
NOT SURE I WOULD HAVE PEGGED YOU AS THE "SUPERHERO" TYPE.
DESPITE RUMORS YOU MIGHT HEAR TO THE CONTRARY...
...I'M MOST DEFINITELY NOT.
SWAMP THING

HOW MANY SHOPS LEFT ON THE LIST?
JUST ONE.
THEN WHAT?

THEN WE'RE GONNA NEED ANOTHER PLAN.
YOU WANNA TELL ME WHY THE HELL YOU'RE INSISTING ON CARRYING THAT SHOE AROUND, JOHN?
YOU NEVER KNOW, MIGHT COME IN HANDY.

YES-- THE GIRL, AND THE ENGLISH HOLE...
YES, THEY WERE IN HERE. ASKING FOR AN OLD JOURNAL, JUST LIKE YOU SAID.

OLDE LONDON TOWNE.
RELAX...
...AND LET THE MARSHMALLOW CLOUDS TAKE YOU AWAY...
WOOOO... HERE IT COMES...
WE BEST DO IT NOW, BEFORE IT'S TOO LATE...

WOoOWWW...

MR. CARVER, I PRESUME?
HEY YOU, WHOEVER YOU ARE, DID YOU HAVE ANY IDEA THAT SUNSETS AREN'T RED, THEY'RE PURPLE AND YELLOW STRIPES?

AND IF YOU LOOK HARD ENOUGH, YOU'LL ALWAYS FIND FLUFFY LITTLE CLOUDS...
...FLUFFY LITTLE CLOUDS.
IT SEEMS AS IF I HAVE COME AT A BAD TIME...

FLUFFY. LITTLE. CLOUDS.

AND JUST WHO THE BLOODY HELL DO YOU THINK YOU ARE?
OH, I KNOW EXACTLY WHO I AM, ***MR. CARVER.***
HOW THE HELL DO YOU KNOW MY NAME?
I KNOW ALL ABOUT YOU, MR. CARVER.
THEN YOU'LL KNOW WHO I BLOODY WORK FOR...
AND WHO MIGHT THAT BE?
THE PRIME MINISTER?
AS BLOODY IF...WOULDN'T CROSS THE ROAD TO PISS ON HER IF SHE WAS ON FIRE.

NO. NO...
NO, I HAVEN'T--NOT YET ANYWAY. I'D THOUGHT I'D WAIT FOR YOU.
BUT I HAVE TO SAY, FROM THE MAN WHO SOLD THE VOTING PUBLIC THE ⊗⊗⊗⊗ SANDWICH THAT IS BREXIT, I WAS EXPECTING FAR, FAR MORE.
BRING HIM IN.
JESUS WEPT.
NO, THAT'S JUST IT--HE DOESN'T. NOT ANYMORE.
CARVER.
HELP ME.
PLEASE...
WHAT IN GOD'S NAME?
I HATE TO BE THE BEARER OF BAD NEWS.
WELL, ACTUALLY, MAYBE IN THIS CASE I DON'T.
BUT IT TURNS OUT THAT THE HOLY CURRENCY YOUR FEATHERED OVERLORD HERE SO RECENTLY USED TO WIELD UNCHECKED POWER ON EARTH...
...ISN'T WORTH THE HUMAN SKIN IT WAS PRINTED ON.

WHAT?
WHAT DO YOU WANT FROM ME?
I WANT YOU TO SAY IT.
CARVER, DON'T...

WHATEVER YOU WANT FROM ME.
I AM YOUR SERVANT.
HOW VERY TOUCHING...

...BUT I NEED A TOKEN, SOMETHING TO PROVE YOUR TRANSFER OF FEALTY.
A SMALL GESTURE THAT LEAVES NO ROOM TO DOUBT YOUR NEWFOUND LOYALTY.

IS WHAT HE'S SAYING THE TRUTH...?
IS HE TELLING THE TRUTH?!
CARVER, I'M BEGGING YOU...
THE CREATOR... I PROMISE YOU... ONE DAY HE WILL BE BACK.

PLEASE... NO...
WHAT HAPPENS NEXT IS TOTALLY UP TO YOU.
BUT PERSONALLY, I'D START WITH THE WINGS.

PARIS.

OH, YOU'RE EARLY.

...YES, BUT OF COURSE, I'M MORE THAN HAPPY TO ACCOMMODATE YOUR SCHEDULE ANY WAY I CAN.

WE ARE?

TAX

NE PAS FUMAR

BY APPOINTMENT ONLY

...YOUR FLIGHT WAS SATISFACTORY, I HOPE?

HE APPEARS TO BE UNDER THE IMPRESSION THAT WE'RE SOMEONE ELSE...

THINK RICH AND RUN WITH IT...

AND WHO AM I TO DISAPPOINT?

FIRST CLASS, IT JUST ISN'T WHAT IT USED TO BE.

AND HERE IN PARIS, HOW DEEP DO YOUR "CONNECTIONS" RUN HERE?

THAT DEPENDS.

PERHAPS ON WHAT WE'RE LOOKING FOR?

...AND HOW MUCH YOU'RE WILLING TO SPEND TO GET IT.

...I LOVE THIS, IT'S JUST PERFECT FOR THE WEST ATRIUM.
PAS SI VITE...SALAUD DE MENTEUR!
<DON'T WORRY, I DOUBT THEY *PARLEZ FRANCAIS*.>
REGARDE.
CONSTANTINE, YOU ☠☠☠☠ JERK!

<I HOPE YOU DROWN FACEDOWN IN YOUR MATCHA LATTES, YOU YUPPIE ONE-PERCENTER SCUM.
<OVER HERE SPENDING TAX BREAKS STOLEN FROM THOSE LESS FORTUNATE THAN YOUR ENTITLED ARSES, WHILE YOUR COUNTRY BURNS AT THE TINY HANDS OF A DEMENTED ORANGE PSYCHOPATH.>

I'M A LITTLE RUSTY, BUT I THINK HE SAID HE HAD AN UNCLE LIVING IN QUEENS.
SEE...
<BUT IF YOU WANT ME TO SWITCH TO ENGLISH I'M SURE THEY'D LIKE TO HEAR THAT THE CLOSEST YOU'VE BEEN TO THE DESERT IS A TWO-WEEK BENDER IN A TUNISIAN CLUB MED...>
<AND THAT THE BRIC-A-BRAC YOU'RE FLOGGING IN HERE AREN'T JUST FAKES, THEY'RE BARELY ONE STEP ABOVE CHINESE-MADE JUMBLE.>
AND WHILE WE MAY NOT HAVE ANY MONEY TO SPEND, I'M PRETTY BLOODY SURE THEY DO.
JUST TELL ME WHAT IT IS YOU'RE LOOKING FOR...
A JOURNAL WAS STOLEN.
STOLEN FROM WHOM?
JACQUES HENRY.
IF I TELL YOU WHERE TO FIND IT, PROMISE ME ONE THING...?
SCOUT'S HONOR, YOU NEVER SEE
AGAIN...

YOU WATCHED ME DROWN IN BAD HIGH SCHOOL FRENCH, WHEN IT TURNS OUT YOU SPEAK IT LIKE A MARSEILLE STREETWALKER.
YOU NEVER ACTUALLY CAME OUT AND ASKED ME, SO I NEVER ACTUALLY TOLD YOU.
DO YOU LIE AWAKE AT NIGHTS THINKING UP NEW WAYS TO BE AN ☠☠☠☠HOLE, OR DOES IT COME NATURALLY?
IT COMES NATURALLY.

YOU WANNA GET RID OF THAT SHOE NOW?
NO.
LIKE I SAID, YOU NEVER KNOW WHEN IT MIGHT COME IN HANDY.

AMERICAN EXCESS CARD, OF COURSE...
IT'S COMFORTING THAT CONSTANTINE HASN'T LOST HIS TOUCH...
SOLD

JUST FOR THE RECORD, I'VE NEVER SET FOOT IN TUNISIA.
BUT A WINTER SEASON BARTENDING AT SANDALS IN SHARM 'EL SHEIKH DOESN'T EXACTLY MAKE YOU LAWRENCE OF ARABIA, NOW DOES IT?

I DID WHAT YOU ASKED. I GAVE THEM THE ADDRESS.
AND?!
AND THEY'RE ON THEIR WAY THERE AS WE SPEAK.

BUT IN THE FUTURE, MISABEL, I'D RATHER YOU DIDN'T PUT ME IN THOSE KINDS OF SITUATIONS.
THEN WHO WOULD PEOPLE LIKE ME GIVE OUR THIRTY PIECES OF SILVER TO?

IT'S DONE.
VERY GOOD.
EGO...
HUBRIS AND ARROGANCE.
WHAT DO YOU WANT?
STRAIGHT TO BUSINESS, I LIKE THAT.
I THINK WE MIGHT HAVE MORE IN COMMON THAN YOU REALIZE, MR. CARVER.
YEAH, DON'T KID YOURSELF, IT'S NOT JUST ME. DEEP DOWN A PART OF ALL OF US LIKES TO THINK THAT WE'RE THE DOG'S BOLLOCKS.
AND DON'T FORGET GOOD OLD "PRIDE." IT MIGHT NOT BE USED AS AN INSULT LIKE THE OTHERS...
WHAT DO YOU WANT FROM ME?
...AND PEOPLE MIGHT EVEN RAG ON ABOUT "PRIDE OF THIS, PRIDE OF THAT," AND MY ADVICE IS AVOID THOSE LIKE THE PLAGUE.
GREENHAM COMMON AIR FORCE BASE.
YOU'RE A LITTLE LATE--ALL THE DREADLOCKED, HAIRY-ARMPITTED LESBOS ARE GONE, ALONG WITH ALL THE NUKES. IT'S BEEN CLOSED FOR 25 YEARS.
THERE'S NOTHING THERE. IT'S A GHOST TOWN.
THEY SAY "PRIDE COMES BEFORE A FALL." WHICH IS TRUE...
...BUT IN MY EXPERIENCE IT'S ALSO USUALLY ACCOMPANIED BY SOME EVIL WHO'S WAITING AROUND THE NEXT CORNER WITH THEIR LEG OUT JUST TO WATCH YOU FALL ON YOUR ARSE.
EXACTLY. IT' PERFECT...

TELL ME.
TELL ME ABOUT SOLOMON?
A TRICK IS A TRICK, IS A CON, IS A DOUBLE CROSS.
BUT SEDUCTION IS A DIFFERENT BEAST.
NO. FOR THAT YOU WILL HAVE TO DO BETTER...SHOW ME YOU CAN LEARN.
AND UNTIL YOU DO, I WANT TO TALK ABOUT DJINN.
BORN OF A SMOKELESS FLAME...
...AND UNRESTRAINED BY PHYSICS IN THE WAY MERE MORTALS ARE.
TO CATCH ONE YOU HAVE TO GO FURTHER--PAST WHAT COMES EASILY TO YOU, MERCURY.
UNGH
HOW? HOW DO I DO THAT?
A SEDUCTION IS A CON YOU CAN SEE COMING RIGHT AT YOU.
AND DEEP DOWN YOU KNOW SOMEONE IS GETTING ONE OVER ON YOU.
MAYBE I WAS MISTAKEN ABOUT YOU.
MAYBE THIS ISN'T WHERE YOU BELONG.
MAYBE YOU'RE SIMPLY NOT STRONG ENOUGH FOR THIS...
URGHHH...
DON'T PATRONIZE ME...
MAYBE I WAS WRONG AND YOU'RE DESTINED TO THE SAME FATE AS YOUR MOTHER...?
DON'T YOU EVER, EVER DARE BRING MY MOTHER INTO THIS...
BUT IF THEY'RE SAYING ALL THE RIGHT THINGS, YOU JUST CHOOSE NOT TO CARE.

YOU DID IT!
YOU CAUGHT A DJINN.

SO TELL ME WHAT SOLOMON HAD THE DJINN BUILD FOR HIM.
WE BUILT HIM A MACHINE.
WHAT KIND OF MACHINE?

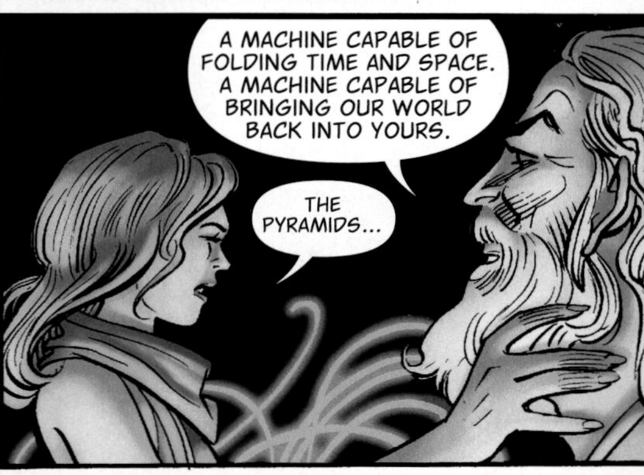
A MACHINE CAPABLE OF FOLDING TIME AND SPACE. A MACHINE CAPABLE OF BRINGING OUR WORLD BACK INTO YOURS.
THE PYRAMIDS...

YES, THE PYRAMIDS.
BUT THE MACHINE WAS NEVER COMPLETED--IT NOW LIES IN RUINS.
YOU'RE GETTING STRONGER.

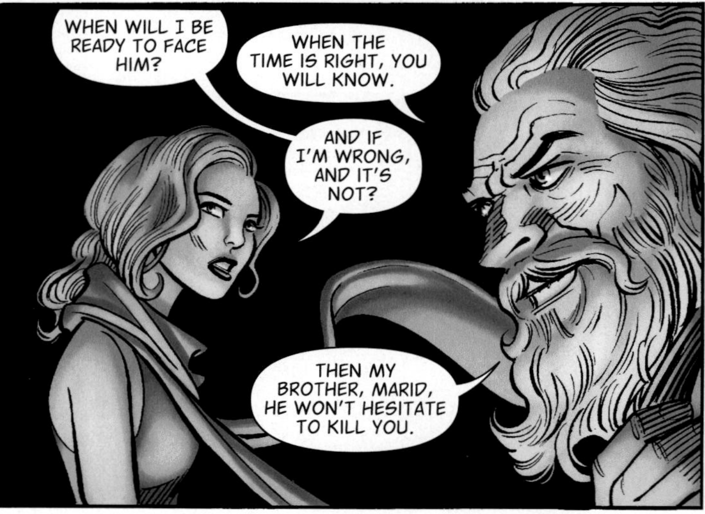
WHEN WILL I BE READY TO FACE HIM?
WHEN THE TIME IS RIGHT, YOU WILL KNOW.
AND IF I'M WRONG, AND IT'S NOT?
THEN MY BROTHER, MARID, HE WON'T HESITATE TO KILL YOU.

ADNAN, HE'S RE-BUILDING SOLOMON'S MACHINE, ISN'T HE?

IT'S NOT LIKE IT'S FARNBOROUGH, OR THE BONNYBRIDGE JOB, GOD FORBID.
I'M GIVING YOU TWO WEEKS TOPS.
IT'S GONNA TAKE US A MONTH JUST TO CLEAR THE SITE.
WORK 'EM AROUND THE CLOCK. DOUBLE RATE.
BUT IF I FIND OUT ANY OF YOUR GUYS HAVE BEEN WHISPERING IN THEIR UNION REPS' SHELL-LIKES IT'S YOUR WRINKLED OLD KNACKERS I'M GONNA BE WEARING AS A MATCHING PAIR.
AS MUCH AS IT WARMS THE COCKLES TO SEE WESTMINSTER HASN'T CHANGED YOU, CARVER, I'VE GOTTA SAY THIS ONE HAS ME SCRATCHING MY HEAD.
THE SMOKELESS FIRE
PART 1
WRITER: SIMON OLIVER PENCILLER: DAVIDE FABBRI
INKER: JOSÉ MARZAN JR.
COLORISTS: CARRIE STRACHAN WITH TONY AVIÑA LETTERING: SAL CIPRIANO
COVER ARTIST: RILEY ROSSMO
ASSOCIATE EDITOR: JESSICA CHEN EDITOR: KRISTY QUINN
GROUP EDITOR: JIM CHADWICK
THAT IF YOU TOLD ME, YOU'D HAVE TO KILL ME?
YOU REALLY IN YOUR *WILDEST* DREAMS THINK I'D STOOP SO LOW AS TO GET MY HANDS DIRTY ON AN OLD NAVVY LIKE YOU?
NO, I'M SURE YOU'VE GOT PLENTY OF PEOPLE WILLING TO GET THEIR HANDS DIRTY.
BELIEVE ME, FOR ONCE YOU REALLY HAVE NO IDEA.
HIGHLY RESTRICTED AREA
MINISTRY OF DEFENSE
JUST REMEMBER WHAT I SAID.

IT AIN'T LIKE IT'S YOUR FIRST JAMBOREE.
ASK NO QUESTIONS.
AND YOU'LL TELL ME NO LIES.
DRAW
VETCOR D
PROJE
TECHNICAL REQUIREMENTS
PARIS
THIS PLACE WAS TO PARIS WHAT ARMPITS WERE TO BRIGITTE BARDOT.
EVERYONE HAD THEM, JUST WASN'T THE FIRST THING THAT SPRUNG TO MIND...
I'M TELLING YOU, CONSTANTINE, WHEN IT COMES TO PISS MY NOSE DOESN'T TELL A LIE. WE'VE PASSED THIS STAIRWELL THREE TIMES ALREADY.
SHHHHH.
BOOMM
BOOOMMM
AND MY EARS NEVER LIE. HEAR THAT?
BOOMM
BUT IT WAS WHERE OUR SEARCH FOR THE THIEF ON THE ROOF, HENRY'S MISSING JOURNAL, THE ROUTE TO THE LOST CITY OF UBAR, AND THE TRAIL OF ABBY ARCANE HAD LED US.
BUT THEN AGAIN--SUPPOSE YOU DON'T HAVE ARMS. ARE THEY STILL CALLED ARMPITS, OR ARE THEY SOMETHING ELSE?
THAT IS WHAT WE'RE LOOKING FOR.

BACK IN LIVERPOOL, THESE PLACES WERE CALL THE "BLUES."
ILLEGAL CLUBS--USED TO RAGE TILL THE SUN CAME UP OR THE ROZZERS RISKED BREAKING DOWN THE DOOR.
HATE TO BREAK IT TO YOU, BUT THAT WAS A LONG TIME AGO AND WE'RE A LONG WAY FROM THE MERSEY, DOROTHY.
PARIS

I KNOW IT'S THE ADDRESS HE GAVE US, BUT YOU SURE ABOUT THIS?
THE ONLY PEOPLE IN THIS WORLD WHO ARE SURE ABOUT ANYTHING ARE GAMBLERS OR FOOLS.
AND RIGHT NOW, WHICH ARE WE?

YOU HAVE A BETTER IDEA?
WHAT HAVE WE GOT TO LOSE?

JOHNNY BLOODY CONSTANTINE. AS I LIVE AND HE STILL BREATHES.

JUST TRY NOT TO STAND OUT LIKE A VIRGIN AT A GANGBANG.
I DON'T EVEN WANT TO START GETTING MY HEAD AROUND WHAT THAT'S SUPPOSED TO MEAN.
RECOGNIZE ANYONE FROM THE ROOF?
NO. NOT YET.
MAYBE WE SHOULD LEAVE A TRAIL OF BREADCRUMBS.
SMILE A LITTLE...
...PRETEND LIKE YOU'RE HAVING FUN, EVEN IF YOU'RE NOT.
AND WHATEVER HAPPENS, DON'T LOOK ANYONE IN THE EYE.
SO PRETTY MUCH LIKE EVERY NIGHT OUT I'VE EVER HAD NORTH OF THE WATFORD GAP?
BINGO.
WHAT IS IT?
MERCURY?
SOMEONE HERE, THEY ALREADY KNOW YOUR NAME...
IT'S A TRICK. WE'VE BEEN SET UP.
NO. NO WAY.
"NO WAY" WHAT?
THAT SOMEONE'S EXPECTING US?
OR THE FACT THAT MISABEL PLAYED US LIKE A CHEAP VIOLIN?
BECAUSE EITHER WAY I'M NOT ABOUT TO HANG AROUND TO FIND OUT.
BUT IT WASN'T "US," IT WAS ME.
AND MISABEL KNEW JUST THE TUNE SHE NEEDED TO PLAY TO GET ME HERE.
AND HERE I WAS, WITH BELLS ON.

JOHN CONSTANTINE!
MERCURY...
...GET OUT, GET WAY, AND WHATEVER YOU DO--DON'T LOOK BACK.
CONSTANTINE, WHAT ARE THEY?
MISABEL SAID YOU WOULD COME.
WHAT THE HELL ARE THEY?!
SORRY, I GOT THE "JOHN," WHAT WAS THE OTHER BIT? "CONSTIPATE"?
SHE SAID TO EXPECT AN ENGLISHMAN...
AND I'D BE THE FIRST TO ADMIT THAT TO THE UNTRAINED EYE WE ALL LOOK ALIKE.
...WEARING A DIRTY TRENCH COAT.
DIDN'T YOU HEAR? THEY'RE MAKING A COMEBACK, ALL THE RAGE.
AND THAT YOU WOULD BE AN ARSEHOLE.
SHE DID, DID SHE?
NO MORE GAMES. I KNOW YOU'RE CONSTANTINE.
NO, MATE, THE TRUTH'S RIGHT HERE IN THE JAWLINE. I'M WAY MORE HANDSOME.
YOU LIE.
ONLY WHEN MY LIPS ARE MOVING.
JOHN, I'M NOT GOING ANYWHERE UNTIL YOU TELL ME WHAT THEY ARE.

SHE PROMISED US A WORTHY QUARRY...
...NOT A CLOWN...
...AND DEFINITELY *NOT* WHATEVER YOU ARE.
LYCANS... WEREWOLVES. THEY'RE BLOODY WEREWOLVES, MERCURY.
CRIKEY...
APRES EUX!
AFTER THEM.

FOR ONCE MAYBE YOU SHOULD HAVE LISTENED TO ME?
FIRST TIME FOR EVERYTHING.

THIS WAY...
SORTIE
KILL

YOU WERE PROMISED TO US, JOHN CONSTANTINE...

WELL YOU'LL JUST HAVE TO CATCH ME FIRST...

JOHN, YOU'VE NEVER SPENT MUCH TIME AROUND FARMS, HAVE YOU...?
NO. BUT GO ON, WHY DO YOU ASK?
BECAUSE I'VE GOT THIS DISTINCT FEELING...

OF WHAT EXACTLY?

...THAT WE'RE BEING HERDED.

HERDED TOWARDS WHAT?

THEIR KILLING FIELDS...

EVER HAD ONE OF "THOSE" FRIENDS?
WE WERE JUST WONDERING...
YOU HAVEN'T BY CHANCE STUMBLED ON A STOLEN JOURNAL?
WE KNOW NOTHING OF ANY JOURNAL.
THANKS FOR THAT, AND WE'LL JUST BE ON OUR WAY THEN.
WE ONLY KNOW WHAT MISABEL PROMISED US.
AND, OUT OF CURIOSITY, WHAT MIGHT THAT BE?
YOUR LIVES.
KNEW I SHOULDN'T HAVE ASKED...
YOU KNOW THE KIND.
JOHN CONSTANTINE.
OLDER-- BUT I CAN SEE NO WISER...
THE KIND OF FRIEND WHO ALWAYS LEAVES YOU WITH THE DISTINCT IMPRESSION THAT IT WAS ONLY A MATTER OF TIME...
BLOODY HELL, I DID NOT SEE THAT COMING.
...BEFORE THEY WERE GOING TO TAKE SOME TIME OUT OF THEIR BUSY SCHEDULE TO FINALLY GETTING AROUND TO KILLING YOU?

WELL, PAPA MIDNITE WAS THE POSTER CHILD FOR ONE OF THOSE "FRIENDS."
NICE TO SEE YOU TOO, JOHN.
WHY DON'T THEY ATTACK HIM?
AT LEAST WITH MIDNITE YOU KNEW HE WAS GONNA BE LOOKING YOU RIGHT IN THE EYE WHEN HE DID IT.
SO ON THE BRIGHT SIDE, I GUESS THAT'S A PLUS.
IS HE ONE OF THEM...?
NO, BUT MY GUESS IS DISEMBOWELING THEIR LEADER--
--MAKES HIM THE NEW BOSSMAN AROUND HERE.
WHAT MAKES YOU SO SURE?
I SAW IT ON TV. "PLANET EARTH."
POINT MADE, MIDNITE, HOW ABOUT YOU CALL THEM OFF NOW?
MIDNITE, STOP JERKING AROUND.
NO, CONSTANTINE, THE ONE WHO NEEDS TO STOP JERKING AROUND...
...IS YOU.

I DIDN'T ASK ANY FAVORS.
NO, IT'S TRUE-- YOU DIDN'T.
BUT FOR BETTER OR WORSE, I KNOW YOU, JOHN CONSTANTINE.

I KNOW YOU **WELL**, WOULDN'T YOU SAY?
AND YOU'VE STILL GOT MORE ROUNDABOUT THAT THE ELEPHANT AND CASTLE.
IS THERE A POINT NEEDS GETTING TO?

WOULD THE "GREAT JOHN CONSTANTINE" I ONCE KNEW HAVE EVER FALLEN FOR A TRAP LIKE THIS?
WHAT'S THE MATTER? CAT GOT YOUR TONGUE?

NO PITHY, BITING COMEBACK?

ALL OUT OF TRICKS?
AND OVER THE HILL?
HOW LONG HAVE YOU BEEN FOLLOWING ME?

THE FACT THAT YOU HAVE TO ASK I THINK ANSWERS MY QUESTION.

MAYBE I SHOULD LET THE LYCANS LOOSE, TO FINISH THIS?
BEFORE YOU BECOME AN EMBARRASSMENT TO WHAT YOU ONCE WERE.
YOU DO THAT.
BOTH OF YOU, PUT THEM AWAY AND ZIP IT UP.
GO ON. LET THEM LOOSE.
OR...

BACK OFF, YOU HEARD ME.
MAYBE NOT TODAY, JOHN CONSTANTINE, BUT ONE DAY...

LOOKING FORWARD TO IT, WITH BELLS ON, MATE.

NO NEED TO THANK ME...
...BUT YOU'D BETTER GET YOUR ACT TOGETHER.
AND YOU'D BETTER STOCK UP ON PEDIGREE CHUM, MATE.
'CAUSE I'D HATE TO BE AROUND WHEN THIS LOT SKIPS A MEAL.

WE HAVEN'T BEEN PROPERLY INTRODUCED. I'M MERCURY.
THEY CALL ME PAPA MIDNITE.
YOU SURE YOU DON'T WANT TO TAG ALONG?

QUITE SURE.
BE JUST LIKE THE "GOOD OLD DAYS"?
MERCURY!

MERCURY. ONE WORD OF ADVICE...
I KNOW, NEVER TURN YOUR BACK ON JOHN CONSTANTINE, AND SLEEP WITH ONE EYE OPEN...
NO--I WAS GONNA SAY, WITH JOHN CONSTANTINE, THERE NEVER WERE ANY GOOD OLD DAYS...

SO, THAT WAS, >ERH< SOMETHING.
WHAT NOW?
CONSTANTINE! HOLD UP...
YOU'RE BORN, YOU DO SOME STUFF, YOU START TO TAKE IT ALL FOR GRANTED, AND IF YOU DON'T END UP NAKED FLOATING FACE DOWN IN A SWIMMING POOL, YOU GET TO GROW OLD AND WRINKLED.
CASE STUDY NUMBER ONE--THEIR "SATANIC MAJESTIES" THE ROLLING BLOODY STONES. THEY WERE WILD, DANGEROUS AND UNTAMED.
WELL, AS WILD, DANGEROUS AND UNTAMED AS ANY FIVE YOUNG MEN FROM DARTFORD WOULD EVER BE.
WOULD THEY STILL BE FARTING AROUND WITH THE SAME OLD SONGS, AND GROPING SUPERMODELS WITH THEIR BONY ARTHRITIC FINGERS??
OKAY. MAYBE NOT THE BEST EXAMPLE. MAYBE I SHOULD HAVE GONE WITH THE BAY CITY ROLLERS...

BUT MAYBE UNDER THE VENEER OF BLAGGING AND BRAGGING, I WAS AFRAID TO ADMIT THAT MIDNITE WAS RIGHT?
BERNARD BISTROT

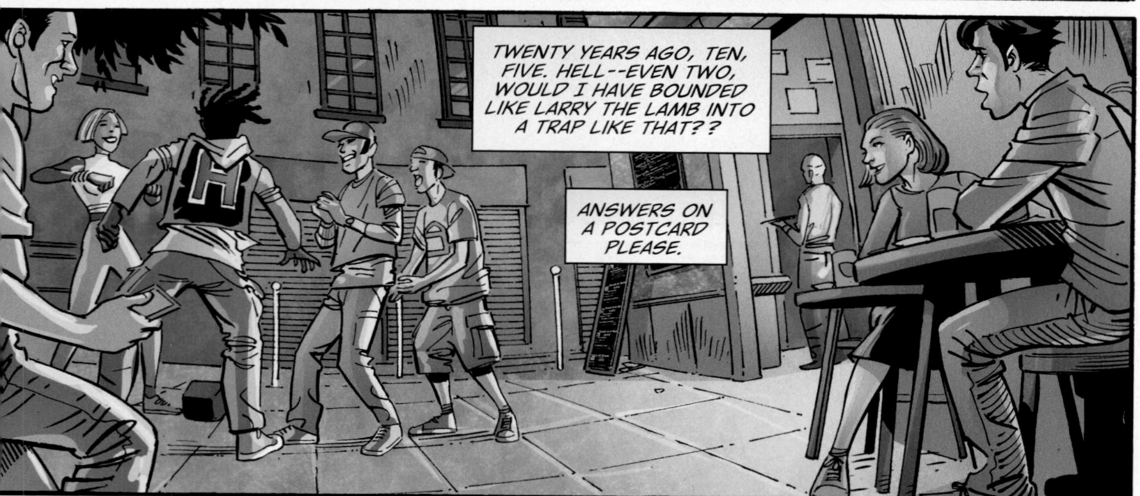
TWENTY YEARS AGO, TEN, FIVE. HELL--EVEN TWO, WOULD I HAVE BOUNDED LIKE LARRY THE LAMB INTO A TRAP LIKE THAT??
ANSWERS ON A POSTCARD PLEASE.

DON'T GET ME WRONG, I KNOW I'D LONG SINCE LEFT THE CHANCE OF DOING A BRIAN JONES AND LEAVING A GOOD-LOOKING CORPSE IN THE REARVIEW.

BUT IT STILL CAME AS A SHOCK WHEN I STARED INTO THE MIRROR AND DIDN'T RECOGNIZE THE OLD MAN STARING BACK.
FROM HERE ON THERE WOULD BE NO MORE SCREW-UPS, OR OWN GOALS IN OVERTIME...

...BECAUSE I AND I ALONE WAS GONNA BE THE ONE WHO GOT TO DECIDE HOW AND WHEN THIS JOURNEY CAME TO AN END.

THEY HAD HELP.
AN UNFORESEEN AND UNAVOIDABLE TURN OF EVENTS.
THEY ESCAPED?
BUT WITHOUT HENRY'S JOURNAL THEY HAVE NO WAY TO FIND UBAR.
AND ARCANE WILL BE SAFE FROM CONSTANTINE AND THE GIRL.

I'M TOLD *YOU* ARE NOW OUR BEST CHANCE OF FINDING THE STOLEN JOURNAL?
DEPENDS...
ON WHAT?
ON WHAT IT'S WORTH TO YOU.

IF CONSTANTINE IS STILL HERE IN PARIS, I CAN HAVE HIM TAKEN CARE OF.
NO. THAT WON'T BE NECESSARY.

I THINK IT'S TIME I TOOK THE JOHN CONSTANTINE ISSUE INTO MY OWN HANDS.

MEANWHILE...
BISTROT St BERNARD
CONSTANTINE... CONSTANTINE. OPEN THE BLOODY DOOR.

JOHN, HAVE YOU FALLEN IN?
BANG BANG

WHHOOA.

WTF ARE YOU UP TO?

WTF AM I DOING?
MAGIC, THAT'S WHAT I'M BLOODY DOING.
BUT YOU SAID YOU COULDN'T DO THE FLYING SHOE AGAIN.
CORRECT.
IF I CAN'T HAVE THE SHOE TAKE US TO ITS OWNER?
THEN I'M GOING TO HAVE THE SHOE'S OWNER COME TO US.
HOW?
I'M A MAGICIAN. REMEMBER?
AND I PROMISE YOU'RE GONNA LOVE THIS. IT'S GONNA BE STRAIGHT OUT OF THE BIG BOY'S BIG BOOK OF MAGIC.
GREAT. AND IF HE DOESN'T SHOW UP?
IF AFTER ALL THIS NO ONE COMES?
THEN WHAT?
THEN, MY DEAR MERCURY, THEN I'M ALL OUT OF IDEAS...
...EVEN REALLY BLOODY STUPID ONES.

JOHN CONSTANTI
BELOVED SON OF
& THOMAS.
HIS BROTHER NOW.

JOHN CONSTANTI
BELOVED SON OF
& THOMAS.
HIS BROTHER NOW.

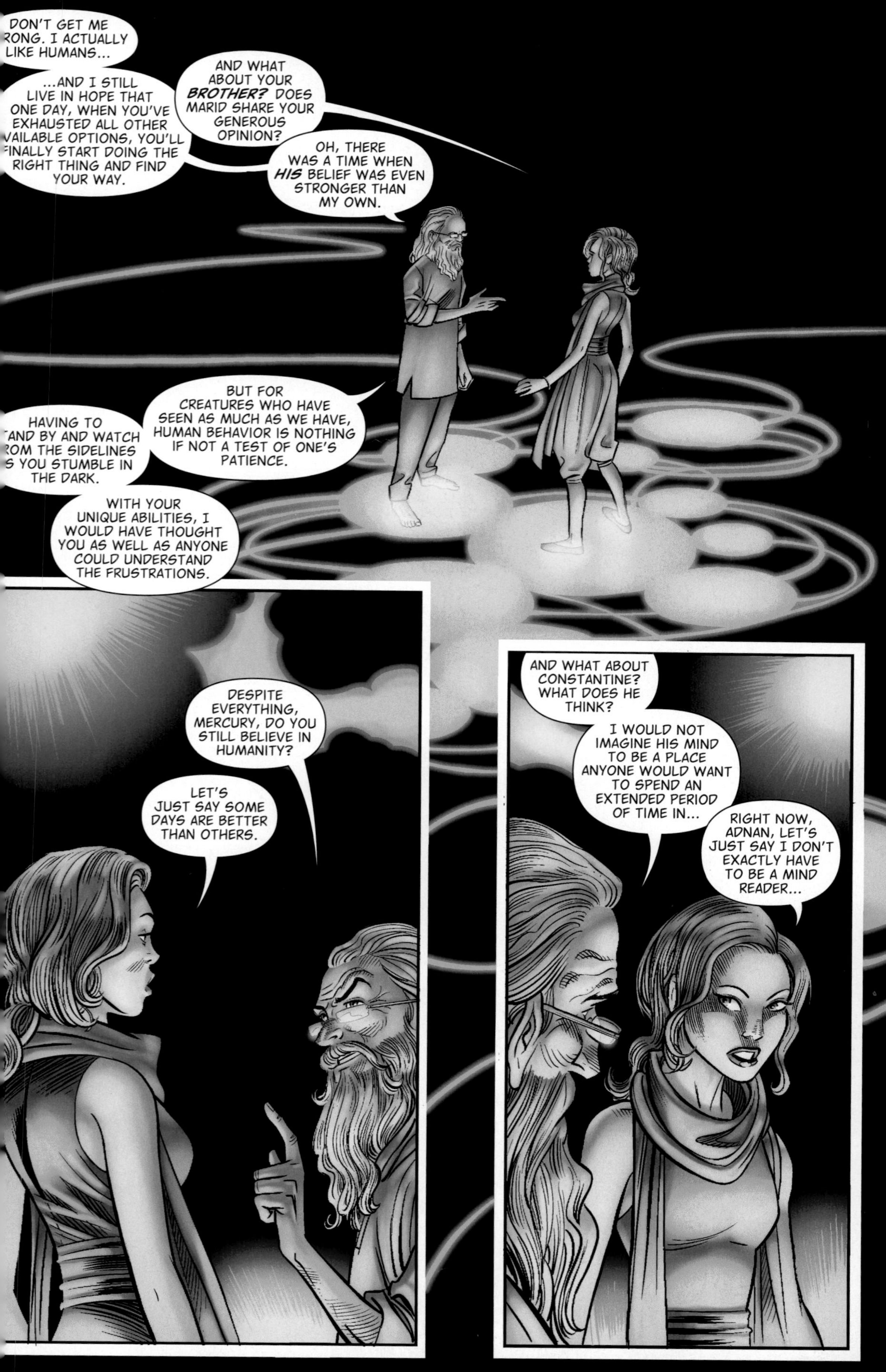

DON'T GET ME RONG. I ACTUALLY LIKE HUMANS...
...AND I STILL LIVE IN HOPE THAT ONE DAY, WHEN YOU'VE EXHAUSTED ALL OTHER VAILABLE OPTIONS, YOU'LL FINALLY START DOING THE RIGHT THING AND FIND YOUR WAY.
AND WHAT ABOUT YOUR ***BROTHER?*** DOES MARID SHARE YOUR GENEROUS OPINION?
OH, THERE WAS A TIME WHEN ***HIS*** BELIEF WAS EVEN STRONGER THAN MY OWN.
BUT FOR CREATURES WHO HAVE SEEN AS MUCH AS WE HAVE, HUMAN BEHAVIOR IS NOTHING IF NOT A TEST OF ONE'S PATIENCE.
HAVING TO TAND BY AND WATCH ROM THE SIDELINES S YOU STUMBLE IN THE DARK.
WITH YOUR UNIQUE ABILITIES, I WOULD HAVE THOUGHT YOU AS WELL AS ANYONE COULD UNDERSTAND THE FRUSTRATIONS.
DESPITE EVERYTHING, MERCURY, DO YOU STILL BELIEVE IN HUMANITY?
LET'S JUST SAY SOME DAYS ARE BETTER THAN OTHERS.
AND WHAT ABOUT CONSTANTINE? WHAT DOES HE THINK?
I WOULD NOT IMAGINE HIS MIND TO BE A PLACE ANYONE WOULD WANT TO SPEND AN EXTENDED PERIOD OF TIME IN...
RIGHT NOW, ADNAN, LET'S JUST SAY I DON'T EXACTLY HAVE TO BE A MIND READER...

"...BECAUSE I KNOW DESPERATION WHEN I SEE IT."
"AND, MERCURY, I'M SURE YOU DON'T NEED ME TO TELL YOU DESPERATE MEN ARE MOST DANGEROUS TO THOSE AROUND THEM."
THE SMOKELESS FIR
PART 5
PARIS, PRESENT DAY.
WRITER: SIMON OLIVER PENCILLER: DAVIDE FA
INKER: JOSÉ MARZA
COLORIST: CARRIE STRA
LETTERING: SAL CIPR
COVER ARTIST: TULA
ASSOCIATE EDITOR: JESSICA
EDITOR: KRISTY
GROUP EDITOR: JIM CHAD
WELL, LAST TIME I CHECKED MY PASSPORT, UNDER PROFESSION HAS ME DOWN AS "MAGICIAN..."
FIRST OFF, WE BOTH KNOW THAT THAT'S A LIE.
MAYBE. BUT I'M TELLING YOU, THIS RIGHT HERE IS GONNA BE STRAIGHT OUT OF THE BUMPER BIG BOY'S WIZARDING BOOK OF BIG BLOODY MAGIC.
AND JUST FOR THE RECORD, I DON'T BELIEVE THAT, EITHER.
SO IF IT DOESN'T WORK, AND HE DOESN'T SHOW UP?
AND WE DON'T FIND HENRY'S JOURNAL AND WE NEVER GET TO ABBY?
Bon Appetit!
CAFE
MY DEAR MERCURY, IN THE WORDS OF THE RECENTLY LATE AND ALWAYS GREAT GEORGIOS KYRIACOS PANAYIOTOU--
"YOU'VE GOTTA HAVE FAITH..."
AND DIDN'T HE ALSO SAY, "GUILTY FEET HAVE GOT NO RHYTHM"?
JUST AS TRUE AND STRANGELY PERTINENT.

BUT SERIOUSLY--IS THIS ALL WE'VE GOT?
A MAGIC DANCING SHOE?
NO, "THE WORLD-FAMOUS DANCING SHOE OF CLICHY SOUS BOIS."
WORD OF THIS CURIOUS WONDER OF THE WORLD WILL SPREAD LIKE WILDFIRE TO EVERY CORNER OF EVERY ARRONDISSEMENT.
AND MARK MY WORDS--PEOPLE WILL COME...
AND IF YOUR ONE-SHOED THIEF ISN'T ONE OF THEM?
THEN FINGERS CROSSED SOMEBODY HE KNOWS WILL CLOCK HIS SHOE AND GO TELL HIM IT'S GONE ALL FRED AND GINGER...
JESUS CHRIST. THAT IS REALLY ALL WE'VE GOT, ISN'T IT?
MAYBE, MAYBE NOT.
BUT IF YOU'RE CREEPY-CRAWLING OUR WAY THROUGH HE RUBBERNECKERS' MINDS...
...WELL IT'S ONLY GOING TO UP THE ODDS, ISN'T IT?
GREAT--A DANCING SHOE AND THE REST IS UP TO ME?
EXACTLY. YOU DOING "YOU," ME DOING "ME."
SKY'S THE LIMIT.
YOU EVER AFRAID THAT YOU MIGHT HAVE JUST TURNED INTO THAT SAD WANKER IN THE PUB?

NOT A MILLION MILES ACROSS THE CITY, AS THE CROW FLIES.
AS MUCH AS HE YELLED, INSULTED AND BERATED THEM, I DON'T THINK THE TRIBESMEN HATED BAPTISTE...

BECAUSE IF THEY DID, I HAVE NO DOUBT THEY WOULD HAVE SLIT HIS THROAT WHILE HE SLEPT...
...AND LET BAPTISTE CHOKE TO DEATH ON HIS OWN WARM BLOOD.

NO, THAT NIGHT THEY LEFT--THEY DIDN'T LEAVE OUT OF HATE.

L' OCCIDENT PETROLEUM CO. ARABIQUE EXPÉDITION, 1936.
THEY LEFT OUT OF FEAR.
PUTAIN...
RÉVEILLEZ-VOUS, RÉVEILLEZ-VOUS... LES SAUVAGES SONT PARTIS...

PUTAIN... VA TE FAIRE FOUTRE....
ARGHHHH...
QUI EST LÀ?
I SAID, WHO'S THERE?

YOU'RE NOT REAL...
YOU'RE NOT REAL...
YOU'RE NOT REAL.
ARGGHHH!
WHAT THE HELL IS THAT?
HOLD ON. I'M COMING...
UHHHF

IT IS TOO LATE.
TOUT EST FINI...
QUE SONT-ILS?

WHAT ARE THEY?
YOU CANNOT SAVE HIM. ONLY YOURSELF.
C'EST FINI.

TELL ME WHAT THEY ARE.
THEY ARE THE DJINN.

...HE IS ALREADY DEAD.

I TOLD YOU, MONSIEUR HENRY--WE HAVE LEFT OUR WORLD BEHIND.
AND WE ARE IN *THEIR* WORLD NOW.
SOME SAY MAYBE OUR WORLD WAS IN FACT THEIRS ALL ALONG.
BANG BANG BANG
DANTE, YOU HOME?
DANTE? WHO'S THAT?
STAY HERE, SAM.

BANG BANG
DANTE, YOU HOME?
DANTE, WHERE DID YOU GET THAT?
...IS IT EVEN REAL?
I TOLD YOU TO GO WAIT ON THE COUCH.
NO FRICKING WAY.
YOU AND ME, THE OLD MAN'S HOUSE. WE PARTED ON BAD TERMS.
PARIS FRANCE
HOW ABOUT WE PUT THAT BEHIND US, LET BYGONES BE BYGONES AND YOU OPEN THE DOOR...
I DON'T TRUST HIM.
YOU ON YOUR OWN, LEON?
ME? I'M ALL ALONE.
HOW ABOUT YOU? JUST LI'L SIS?
WHAT OF IT?
I KNOW YOU AIN'T LIKE US, DANTE...
...ME AND THE BOYS, WE'RE JUST NO-GOOD BANGERS.
BUT NOT YOU, DANTE, YOU GOT BRAINS. YOU GET OUT OF HERE, GIVE THAT LI'L SIS THE LIFE YOU KNOW SHE DESERVES.
ISN'T THAT WHAT YOU WANT?

WHAT DO YOU WANT FROM ME, LEON?
LIKE I ALREADY SAID, IT'S BUSINESS.

YOU GOT SOMETHING I WANT, AND IN RETURN I'M GONNA GIVE YOU ENOUGH MONEY TO START OVER SOME-PLACE A LONG WAY FROM HERE.
I DON'T KNOW WHAT YOU'RE TALKING ABOUT. I AIN'T GOT NO BOOK...
YEAH YOU DO.
THE OLD MAN'S PLACE.

RING ANY BELLS?

THINK OF THAT BOOK AS YOUR GOLDEN TICKET OUT OF HERE, DANTE...

DANTE, DON'T BELIEVE HIM.
HE'S LYING...
SO YOU GONNA OPEN THE DOOR AND GIVE ME THE BOOK OR NOT, DANTE?

DANTE! HE'S LYING...

SAM, YOU MIGHT BE THE BRAINS OF THIS OPERATION. BUT JUST THIS ONCE, I NEED YOU TO LISTEN TO ME.
IT'S YOU AND ME AGAINST THE WORLD. OKAY, PUMPKINHEAD?
OKAY...
NOW LET'S GO SEE IF YOU'RE RIGHT AND HE'S LYING.

DARE I ASK EXACTLY HOW YOU KNOW HOW TO GET UP HERE?
NO. A GIRL'S GOTTA HAVE SOME SECRETS.

HE'S GONE TO GET IT.
NO, HE HASN'T.
LEON, YOU LYING SACK OF SH--
DANTE! IF I CAN'T SAY IT, WHY SHOULD YOU?

WHO'S HE WITH...?
I DON'T KNOW.
COULD THEY BE THE "THINGS" FROM YOUR BOOK?

SNAP

DIDN'T I TELL YOU NOT TO LOOK INSIDE IT...?
I DIDN'T. WELL, JUST A PEEK, WAS ALL...

BRING THEM TO ME.
AND FIND ME THE JOURNAL.

THEY'RE NOT HERE...
I CAN SEE THAT.

PARIS
THIS WAY.

GREAT, BUT WE'VE STILL GOTTA GET DOWN.
I TOLD YOU I HAVE A PLAN.

HOLD TIGHT...
...WE'RE GOING THE WRONG WAY.

DANTE, YOU NEED TO LISTEN TO ME.

ASCENSEUR

ALL RIGHT. YOU WIN--THEY'RE EVERYWHERE, SO HOW ARE WE GONNA GET DOWN?
BY GOING *UP*.

I WAS RIGHT--THEY'D COME TO SEE THE "DANCING SHOE OF CLICHY SOUS BOIS."
BUT THEY'D GROWN SO NUMB TO BOIL-IN-THE-BAG MIRACLES...
...THINGS JUST **ARE**, THE IMPOSSIBLE JUST **HAPPENS**. SO WHY BOTHER ASKING QUESTIONS, IF YOU NO LONGER GIVE TWO ABOUT THE ANSWERS?
THE ORIGINAL SIN. GOOD VERSUS EVIL. HEAVEN AND HELL. WHO GIVES A MONKEY'S?
'CAUSE IF THE DEVIL HIMSELF CAME DOWN AND REVEALED HIMSELF, THESE TOSSERS WOULD PROBABLY LINE UP AROUND THE BLOCK TO MAKE HIM THEIR LEADER.
WHEN YOU CAN BOUNCE A HIGH DEF PHOTO OF YOUR JUNK OFF A SATELLITE ZIPPING ABOVE THE PLANET AND ZAP IT IN THE HANDS OF ANYONE, ANYWHERE ON EARTH...
...WHERE DOES THAT LEAVE "MAGIC"?
MAYBE IT WAS TIME FOR ME TO STOP KICKING AGAINST THE , LET HUMANITY RUN ITS COURSE...
...AND FADE TO BLACK.
JOHN!
HEY, MERC, THAT OLD PSYCHIC POLICE SCANNER OF YOURS AIN'T GOT A TWITCH YET HAS IT?
NO, JOHN-- **BETTER**. YOU BLOODY DID IT...
THE DANCING SHOE'S GONE VIRAL.
AND THAT'S A GOOD THING? RIGHT?

AND DARE I ASK IF YOU'VE DONE THIS BEFORE?
YEAH ALL T TIME
YOU'RE LYING AREN'T YOU?
RIGHT NOW IS THAT A GOOD THING, OR A BAD THING?
LET'S TALK ABOUT THAT LATER.
ARGHHHHH!

DANTE!

SHH, SAM. I'M CHECKING THE COAST IS CLEAR.

JUST REMEMBER THEY'RE MORE AFRAID OF YOU THAN YOU ARE OF THEM.

NOW THAT'S A ⊗⊗⊗⊗ LIE.

SHHHHH

MERDE. WATCH WHERE YOU'RE STEPPING, WEIRDO...
WHO THE HELL ARE YOU, ANYWAY?
WHAT'S HAPPENING OUT THERE?
I DON'T KNOW.
VA TE FAIRE FOUTRE!
FILS DE PUTE!

BRÛLE EN L'ENFER.
OH, I'D LOVE TO. BUT, YOU SEE, HELL WON'T TAKE THE LIKES OF US.
WE'RE GONNA MAKE A RUN FOR IT...
IT'S THEM, ISN'T IT?
THE "ONES" FROM YOUR BOOK...
THIS TIME YOU'VE GOT TO PROMISE TO DO AS I SAY. AND WHATEVER YOU DO--DON'T LOOK BACK.
I PROMISE.

HOLD ON, I'M COMING...
WHAT'S HER NAME?
HER NAME'S CHERIE. AND I'M TELLING YOU, BE NICE.
WELL I JUST WANT TO KNOW HOW COME YOU'VE NEVER MENTIONED THIS "CHERIE" BEFORE...
DANTE, I WASN'T EXPECTING YOU...
CHERIE, WE'RE GONNA NEED SOME-WHERE TO CRASH...
AND WHO'S THIS? YOU NEVER TOLD ME YOU WERE A BABY DADDY?
THIS IS MY SISTER.
COME IN-- DON'T PRETEND LIKE YOU KNOW THE WAY.
SAM TO MY FRIENDS. BUT YOU CAN CALL ME SAMANTHA.
SHE'S JUST A FRIEND.
YOU THINK I'M TOO YOUNG TO KNOW A "BOOTY CALL" WHEN I SEE IT?
DOESN'T MATTER. EITHER WAY YOU'RE STAYING.
FINE, I'LL STAY. BUT I'M ALSO SAYING YOU SHOULDN'T DO IT.
YOU SAW WHAT THEY DID BACK THERE-- YOU SAW.
YOU KNOW WHAT THEY CAN DO.
AND BY DESTROYING THE BOOK, WHAT IF ALL YOU'RE DOING IS SAVING THEM THE TROUBLE?
SAM, I'M IN CHARGE AND THAT'S THE PLAN.
WHAT'S "BOOTY CALL" SQUAWKING ABOUT?
HA... HAHHAA... HA...
HEY GUYS COME CHECK THIS OUT...
GUYS, YOU GOTTA SEE THIS VIDEO.

WHAT'S UP?
'CAUSE IF IT'S ANOTHER VIDEO OF A CAT PLAYING PIANO--?!
NO, DANTE--CHECK IT OUT.

ISN'T THAT YOUR RATTY-ARSED SNEAKER?

YOU GOT DISTRACTED...
YOU LET THEM GET AWAY.

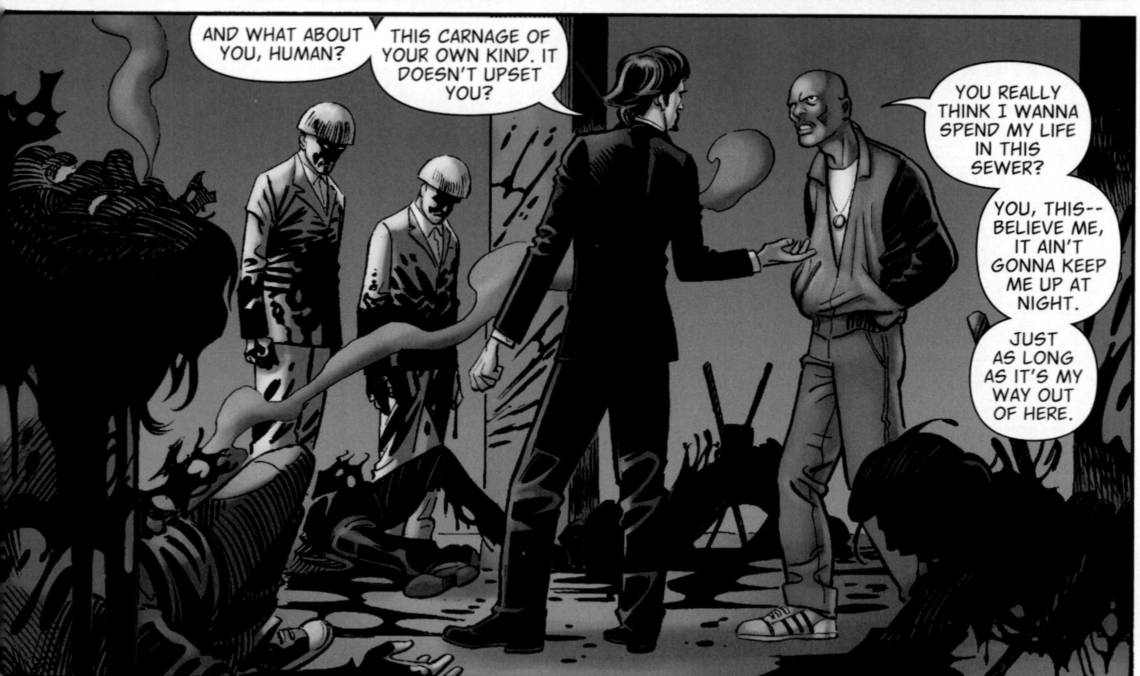
AND WHAT ABOUT YOU, HUMAN?
THIS CARNAGE OF YOUR OWN KIND. IT DOESN'T UPSET YOU?
YOU REALLY THINK I WANNA SPEND MY LIFE IN THIS SEWER?
YOU, THIS--BELIEVE ME, IT AIN'T GONNA KEEP ME UP AT NIGHT.
JUST AS LONG AS IT'S MY WAY OUT OF HERE.

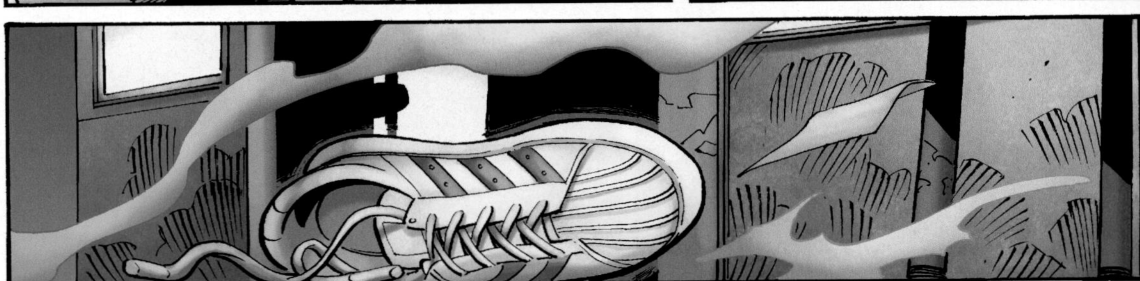

"VIRAL" MY ARSE.

I WASN'T SURE I'D COME.

WELL THAT MAKES TWO OF US.

THE HELLBLAZER

THE HELLBLAZER

PARIS.

THE SMOKELESS FIRE PART 6

WRITER: SIMON OLIVER PENCILLER: DAVIDE FABBRI
INKER: JOSÉ MARZAN JR.
COLORIST: CARRIE STRACHAN
LETTERING: SAL CIPRIANO
COVER ARTIST: TULA LOTAY
ASSOCIATE EDITOR: JESSICA CHEN
EDITOR: KRISTY QUINN
GROUP EDITOR: JIM CHADWICK

SO? WHAT'S YOUR POINT?

I'M JUST TELLING YOU DANTE'S NEVER MENTIONED YOU. NOT ONCE. NOT EVEN IN PASSING.

SO YOU'RE ASSUMING I DON'T MEAN THAT MUCH TO HIM?

AND THEREFORE YOU THINK I'M WHAT? JUST ANOTHER ***BOOTY CALL?***

YOUR WORDS, NOT MINE. BUT I AIN'T GONNA ARGUE.

YOU KNOW WHAT I THINK? I THINK DANTE NEVER MENTIONED YOU BECAUSE HE WAS PROTECTING YOU.
YOUR BROTHER--HE'S A GOOD MAN. THE BEST I KNOW.
NOT THAT THAT'S SAYING MUCH AROUND THESE PARTS.

...AND I KNOW HE WILL DO WHATEVER HE HAS TO DO TO PROTECT HIS LI'L SIS...
...AND MAKE SURE THAT NOTHING BAD *EVER*, EVER HAPPENS TO HER.
OKAY?

YEAH. I'M OKAY.

SO, LET'S TURN THAT FROWN UPSIDE DOWN, SHALL WE?

DINGDONG

DANTE SAID NOT TO OPEN THE DOOR.
CHILL, I'M JUST GOING TO SEE WHO IT IS.

LEON!

WHERE IS THE CHILD?
SHE'S NOT HERE.
COME NOW, IT'S AN EASY QUESTION.
CERTAINLY NOTHING TO LOSE YOUR HEAD OVER.
URGHHH!

RIPPPP

COME ON, COME ON.

WHERE THE HELL IS SHE?
OH, SHE'S STILL HERE.

WE JUST NEED TO FIND HER.

I'M NOT SURE WHAT I'M DOING HERE.
THAT MAKES TWO OF US.

THE MILLION DOLLAR QUESTION. DID YOU BRING IT?

FIRST THINGS FIRST. I WANNA KNOW WHO THE HELL YOU ARE.
WHO *I* AM?

THAT'S A BIG QUESTION TO BE ASKING SO SOON AFTER CLOSING TIME.
SO WHY DON'T YOU JUST GIVE ME THE BOOK?
AND IN RETURN I PINKIE PROMISE WE'LL CIRCLE BACK, SO TO SPEAK, AND TACKLE MY *CURRICULUM VITAE* AT A MORE OPPORTUNE TIME.

...THE BROTHER WITH THE GUN GETS TO CALL THE SHOTS.
SO. FIRST OFF, JUST WHO THE ARE YOU?
WOW, THAT ESCALATED QUICKLY.

LIKE YOU SAID, IT'S LATE...
AND FROM WHERE I'M STANDING YOU'RE JUST ANOTHER WHITE-BOY "ROSBIF" ⊗⊗⊗⊗ ⊗⊗⊗⊗ BEGGING FOR A CAP IN HIS ASS.
A STUDENT OF BOTH THE HUMAN CONDITION AND TUPAC'S GREATEST HITS. QUITE THE RENAISSANCE MAN, AREN'T WE?
CONSTANTINE, DON'T...

DANTE. THE CREATURES, THE ONES IN THE BOOK--WE BOTH KNOW THEY'RE REAL AND THEY'RE HERE.
TRUST ME, WE'RE NOT GOING TO DESTROY OR LET THAT BOOK FALL INTO THE WRONG HANDS.
NOW, MY FRIEND HERE MIGHT BE AN ☠☠☠HOLE, BUT WE'RE GOING TO DO THE RIGHT THING.

HOW THE HELL DOES SHE KNOW MY NAME?
OH, YOU'LL GET USED TO THAT.
BUT ABOVE ALL...
...WE'RE GOING TO MAKE SURE NOTHING BAD HAPPENS TO YOUR LI'L SIS. YOUR LI'L PUMPKINHEAD.

BERNARD
SHE'S A ☠☠☠ WITCH...
CLOSE. SHE'S A MIND-READER, BORN UNDER A WANING MOON, WITH A TOUCH OF THE GYPSY ROSE LEES.
IT'S HER PARTY TRICK.

AND WHAT'S YOURS?
ME? I CAN FART AT WILL.
IS HE SERIOUS?

LIKE I ALREADY TOLD YOU, HE'S AN ☠☠☠HOLE.
I WOULDN'T JOKE ABOUT A THING LIKE THAT.
IF HE'S SUCH AN ☠☠☠HOLE, THEN WHY SHOULD I TRUST HIM?

BECAUSE YOU'D BE SURPRISED HOW FAR BEING AN ☠☠☠HOLE HAS GOT ME...
A DIRTY RAINCOAT, THE STENCH OF LAST NIGHT'S LIQUOR AND STALE CIGARETTES.
NEVER JUDGE A BOOK BY ITS COVER...AND ON THE SUBJECT OF WHICH...
JUDGING BY YOUR REACTION, I'M GUESSING YOU'VE SEEN FIRST HAND WHAT *THE DJINN* CAN DO.
YOU'RE NOT EXACTLY IN A POSITION TO PICK AND CHOOSE YOUR CAVALRY...

THINK OF US AS KINDRED SPIRITS.
BROTHERS IN ARMS. STRANGE BEDFELLOWS.
SU CASA ES ME CASA.
AND YOU TRUST HIM?
ERH, SURE. I TRUST HIM.
I MEAN ***REALLY*** TRUST HIM. TRUST HIM WITH YOUR LIFE "TRUST HIM..."?

REALLY? THIS IS THE ONLY WAY?

LEON WILL HAVE PUT A PRICE ON MY HEAD.

WE GET SPOTTED WALKING IN THE FRONT...

...AND TRUST ME, WE ***WILL***...

...THEN BOOK OR NO BOOK, IT DON'T MATTER A DAMN, 'CAUSE WE AIN'T GETTING OUTTA HERE. NOT ALIVE.

COME ON, JOHN, THERE'S NO CHOICE. YOU GOTTA DO IT.

YEAH, YEAH.

WOOOOW...
SEE, THE OLD MAN'S STILL GOT IT...
DIDN'T ANYONE SEE THAT?
YEAH, I SAW IT, GOLD STAR FOR JOHN. NOW COME ON.
ARE YOU FRICKING KIDDING ME? I THOUGHT THAT WAS IT...
YOU DONE?
YOU WANT TO SIT THIS ONE OUT?
NO, I AIN'T DONE. NOT YET.
I WAS THE ONE WHO GOT TO DECIDE HOW AND WHERE THIS ALL ENDS. AND I WASN'T READY, NOT YET.

WHERE'S SHERPA BLOODY TENZIG WHEN YOU NEED HIM?

HERE IT IS...

HERE. ALL YOURS...TAKE IT.

JOHN. YOU WANNA TAKE A LOOK?

YEAH, ONCE I GET USED TO THE ALTITUDE. IS THE AIR THINNER? OR IS IT JUST ME?

ECAUSE I'D LLY HATE TO K I CAME ALL IS WAY FOR OTHING...

MR. JOHN CONSTANTINE, I PRESUME?

THE JOURNAL, IF YOU DON'T MIND.

TAKE IT FROM ME-- I TOOK A QUICK GANDER, AND UNLESS YOU HAPPEN TO HAVE A VESTED INTEREST IN BATHHOUSES AND VICTORIA SPONGE RECIPES, I'D TAKE A PASS.

AS USUAL, PLAYING DUMB, LETTING THE MARK UNDERESTIMATE HIM WHILE HE PLOTS HIS NEXT MOVE.

WELL, IT'S NOT GOING TO WORK THIS TIME.

THE JOURNAL, IF YOU PLEASE...

GET YOUR DIRTY HANDS OFF OF ME.
SAM.
DANTE, DON'T!

YOU HURT...

...A HAIR ON HER HEAD...

...AND I SWEAR I'LL--
HE DOES THAT A LOT. YOU'LL GET USED TO IT.

AND YOU'LL DO...
...WHAT, EXACTLY?
PHOOZM

DANTE, NO!
HE'S ALIVE.
FOR NOW. AND THE SAME WILL GO FOR HIS SISTER...
...AS LONG AS YOU GIVE ME THAT JOURNAL.
THE JOURNAL, THE ROAD TO UBAR.
THEY MUST BE IMPORTANT TO YOUR PLANS.
A LOOSE --NOTHING E, NOTHING LESS.
AND ABBY ARCANE? IS SHE A LOOSE END, TOO?
ON'T H YOUR LUCK.
DANTE!
OH YES, I KNOW ALL ABOUT YOU AND YOUR ORIGINAL SIN, JOHN CONSTANTINE.
A SEEDY NIGHTCLUB IN NEWCASTLE, TRADED IN FOR A SEEDY ROOFTOP ON THE WRONG SIDE OF PARIS.
LET ME GO YOU HOLES.
I'M NOT SURE IF THAT MADE IT BETTER OR WORSE.
I KNOW WHAT YOU'RE THINKING.
BUT YOU CAN'T JUST GIVE HIM THE JOURNAL.
I'M NOT GOING TO.
JOHN, WHAT THE HELL ARE YOU DOING?
YOU'VE GOT NO CARDS LEFT TO PLAY.
YES, I HAVE.

RULE NUMBER ONE, MERC. IN FUTURE DON'T MAKE A PROMISE YOU CAN'T KEEP.
BUT YOU DO THAT ALL THE TIME?
EXACTLY. YOU DON'T WANT TO BE LIKE ME, DO YOU?
TAKE THIS.
FIND ABBY, AND FINISH THIS.
AND WHAT ABOUT YOU?
DON'T WORRY ABOUT ME.
JOHN, DON'T.
SO, WHAT'S IT TO BE?
YOU LET THEM LEAVE, WITH THE BOOK.
AND IN RETURN, WHAT DO I GET?
YOU GET ME.

KILL HIM!

DON'T TRUST HIM.
YOU HEARD HER. HE HAS NOTHING...NO CARDS LEFT TO PLAY.
WHY SHOULDN'T I BELIEVE HIM?

KILL HIM...
YOU DON'T KNOW HIM LIKE I DO. IT'S A TRICK.
WHY NOW, CONSTANTINE?
AFTER ALL THESE YEARS, WHY WOULD YOU SURRENDER LIKE THIS?

WHY NOW?
'CAUSE IT'S TIME.

AND JUST LIKE THAT, "THE GREAT JOHN CONSTANTINE" LAYS DOWN HIS LIFE AT MY FEET.

CALL IT BRAGGING RIGHTS.
NOT EXACTLY THE BOAST IT ONCE WAS, NOW IS IT?

MAYBE.

BUT YOU'LL FIND IT'S STILL GOOD FOR A FREE ROUND IN SOME PARTS.

URGHHHH
COME ON, LET'S GET OUT OF HERE.
IT MIGHT HAVE BEEN PARIS.
BUT IT DIDN'T MATTER.
JUST LIKE IT DIDN'T MATTER HOW FAR OR HOW FAST YOU RAN.
WALK INTO THE LIGHT.

BECAUSE THERE'S ALWAYS A PERVERSE SYMMETRY AT PLAY.
WALK INTO THE LIGHT.

LIFE HAS A NASTY HABIT OF TAKING YOU RIGHT BACK TO WHERE IT ALL STARTED.
WALK INTO THE LIGHT.

ONLY THIS TIME, I WAS TRADING MY LIFE TO SAVE AN INNOCENT.
WALK INTO THE LIGHT.

I WAS THE ONE BEING CONDEMNED TO AN ETERNITY IN HELL.

DON'T ASK ME HOW, BUT IT WORKED.
YOUR FRIENDS HAV TAKEN THE JOURNAL...

...I THINK THEY THINK YOU'RE DEAD. I KNOW *I* DID.
BUT DON'T WORRY, I'M SURE SOMEWHERE ON THE ROAD TO UBAR, MARID WILL FIND THEM AGAIN.

I'LL PROBABLY NEVER KNOW WHAT TRICK YOU MIGHT HAVE HAD UP YOUR SLEEVE.

BUT IF BY SOME SMALL CHANCE I WAS WRONG AND YOU DIDN'T?

AND ALL THIS WAS JOHN CONSTANTINE'S BIG CHANCE AT A FINAL REDEMPTION.
I'M JUST HAPPY I COULD BE HERE TO SCREW IT UP FOR YOU.

TWO MONTHS LATER. NORMANDY.

SOMEONE ONCE SAID THAT THE ONLY DIFFERENCE BETWEEN ME AND THE DEVIL...

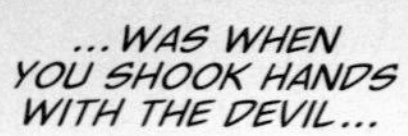
...WAS WHEN YOU SHOOK HANDS WITH THE DEVIL...

...YOU DIDN'T HAVE TO COUNT YOUR FINGERS AFTERWARD.
MON BOUTEILLE, VA TE FAIRE FOUTRE...

OÙ ALLEZ-VOUS...
THE ONE TIME I'D ACTUALLY COME CLEAN AND TOLD THE TRUTH?

NOBODY BELIEVED ME.

AND AS FOR THE "WHITE LIGHT" BIT?
I MADE THAT PART UP.
A LITTLE POETIC LICENSE.
WHAT I LIKE TO THINK OF AS "SUPERNATURAL COMFORT FOOD." SOMETHING TO PUT YOU ALL AT EASE AND MAKE YOU FEEL BETTER ABOUT THE DEATH THAT--LIKE IT OR NOT--IS COMING FOR ALL OF US.
IF YOU REALLY WANT TO KNOW WHAT'S WAITING FOR YOU ON THE "OTHER SIDE"?
YOU'RE GONNA HAVE TO STOP RELYING ON ME...
...AND PULL YER FINGER OUT OF YER ARSE AND GO AND FIND OUT FOR YOURSELF.
NEXT: LONDO

THE HELLBLAZER

VARIANT COVER GALLERY

THE HELLBLAZER #7 by YASMINE PUTRI

THE HELLBLAZER #8 by YASMINE PUTRI

THE HELLBLAZER #9 by YASMINE PUTRI

THE HELLBLAZER #11 by YASMINE PUT

THE HELLBLAZER #12 by YASMINE PUTRI